"Christi is our preeminent hope! Kevi
of this grand statement from Colossi
though, he exegetically, theologically, a
to our daily life 'in Christ.' We live in a l.
death, resurrection, and ascension of our God and King, Jesus Christ, who is
not only preeminent but also sufficient. We have everything we need in him
during our pilgrimage here on earth: faith, love, and hope—even in the most
dire circumstances. What McFadden shows his readers is the glorious power
of a hope-filled gospel that definitively proves one thing: 'No one is without
hope, and we should never give up hope.' This book will water the garden of
your heart with Christ, the hope of glory."

David E. Briones, Associate Professor of New Testament, Westminster
Theological Seminary

"Paul's letter to the Colossians is focused on the supremacy, rule, and glory of
Christ and all that he achieved through the cross. Kevin McFadden faithfully
unpacks these themes so that our eyes are drawn to Christ, in whom are hidden all the treasures of wisdom and understanding that far outstrip the empty
philosophies of this world. McFadden's book is not just a helpful resource on
Colossians and Philemon for students and pastors; it will also encourage the
heart of anyone wanting to dig deeper into the wonders of Christ."

Claire Smith, New Testament scholar; author, *God's Good Design:
What the Bible Really Says about Men and Women*

"In this volume, Kevin McFadden has made an invaluable contribution to work
on Colossians and Philemon. It's written clear enough for everyone to benefit
and substantial enough to satisfy scholars and students of New Testament
theology. More importantly, McFadden not only lays out interpretive options
but also makes persuasive cases on some exegetically difficult passages—all
thoughtfully presented. This book is already helping me understand Paul better
in these two letters, and for that, I am grateful."

Robert S. Kinney, Director of Ministries, Charles Simeon Trust; Priest,
Christ Church, Vienna, Austria

"Kevin McFadden has written a clear, accessible, exegetically faithful, and theologically rich book on Colossians and Philemon, pointing us as readers to our ultimate hope in Christ. Those who read this book may not agree with each of McFadden's exegetical moves or with every theological insight, but readers should draw much encouragement from the important theme in his exposition that the believer's life is indeed hidden in Christ."

Jarvis J. Williams, Professor of New Testament Interpretation,
The Southern Baptist Theological Seminary

Hidden with Christ in God

New Testament Theology

Edited by Thomas R. Schreiner and Brian S. Rosner

Hidden with Christ in God

A Theology of Colossians and Philemon

Kevin W. McFadden

∷ CROSSWAY®

WHEATON, ILLINOIS

Library of Congress Cataloging-in-Publication Data

Names: McFadden, Kevin W., 1980– author.
Title: Hidden with Christ in God : a theology of Colossians and Philemon / Kevin W. McFadden.
Description: Wheaton, Illinois : Crossway, 2023. | Series: New Testament theology | Includes bibliographical references and index.
Identifiers: LCCN 2022051501 (print) | LCCN 2022051502 (ebook) | ISBN 9781433576560 (trade paperback) | ISBN 9781433576577 (pdf) | ISBN 9781433576591 (epub)
Subjects: LCSH: Hope—Religious aspects—Christianity. | Jesus Christ.
Classification: LCC BV4638 .M454 2023 (print) | LCC BV4638 (ebook) | DDC 234/.25—dc23/eng/20230615
LC record available at https://lccn.loc.gov/2022051501
LC ebook record available at https://lccn.loc.gov/2022051502

For my sister Kelley†
Now and ever we confess
Christ our hope in life and death

Contents

Series Preface

THERE ARE REMARKABLY FEW TREATMENTS of the big ideas of single books of the New Testament. Readers can find brief coverage in Bible dictionaries, in some commentaries, and in New Testament theologies, but such books are filled with other information and are not devoted to unpacking the theology of each New Testament book in its own right. Technical works concentrating on various themes of New Testament theology often have a narrow focus, treating some aspect of the teaching of, say, Matthew or Hebrews in isolation from the rest of the book's theology.

The New Testament Theology series seeks to fill this gap by providing students of Scripture with readable book-length treatments of the distinctive teaching of each New Testament book or collection of books. The volumes approach the text from the perspective of biblical theology. They pay due attention to the historical and literary dimensions of the text, but their main focus is on presenting the teaching of particular New Testament books about God and his relations to the world on their own terms, maintaining sight of the Bible's overarching narrative and Christocentric focus. Such biblical theology is of fundamental importance to biblical and expository preaching and informs exegesis, systematic theology, and Christian ethics.

The twenty volumes in the series supply comprehensive, scholarly, and accessible treatments of theological themes from an evangelical perspective. We envision them being of value to students, preachers, and interested laypeople. When preparing an expository sermon series, for example, pastors can find a healthy supply of informative commentaries, but there are few options for coming to terms with the overall teaching of each book of the New Testament. As well as being useful in sermon and Bible study preparation, the volumes will also be of value as textbooks in college and seminary exegesis classes. Our prayer is that they contribute to a deeper understanding of and commitment to the kingdom and glory of God in Christ.

We live in a world that is "spiritual" but also wants a religion that is "practical." Paul instructs us about true spirituality and concrete practicality in both Colossians and Philemon. There is no true spirituality that isn't Christ-centered, for any claim of being spiritual is false if the person and work of Jesus are shunted aside. After all, Jesus is fully divine, and believers are reconciled to God and forgiven of their sins through his death and resurrection, and no pathway to God exists outside of Christ. Any attempt to reach the highest heavens and to uncover the greatest mysteries is futile, counterproductive, and a testament to human pride if it skirts around or ignores the truth that all of God's mysteries are ours in Jesus Christ. He is the path to wisdom, knowledge, and understanding. The apostle Paul, however, doesn't communicate what it means to be a believer in abstract terms. He unfolds in Colossians, with practical instructions, what it means to live a Christ-centered life. In the tense situation between Philemon and Onesimus Paul delicately negotiates the relationship between the master and the slave, affirming the dignity, personhood, and value of Onesimus in the process. Kevin McFadden deftly handles all these matters in this pithy and insightful exposition of hope that animates believers. Here the riches of Colossians and Philemon are opened for readers, and our hope and prayer is that we will be reminded afresh that Christ is sufficient for every need.

Thomas R. Schreiner and Brian S. Rosner

Preface

THIS BOOK IS A BRIEF BUT COMPREHENSIVE SUMMARY of the theology of Colossians and Philemon. These two letters are often grouped together because they were written at the same time and sent together to the church at Colossae, which likely met in Philemon's house (Philem. 2). My goal in writing this book has been to supplement the many excellent commentaries on these letters with a readable overview of their major themes. My hope is that pastors and Bible teachers beginning a series on Colossians or Philemon could read this book in a weekend and come away with the big picture of Paul's teaching in these letters. Those working on Colossians should read the first four chapters, and those working on Philemon should read the fifth chapter. I also hope that the book will be of some benefit to scholars and seminary students, although experts will see that my reading of the massive amount of secondary literature on these letters was necessarily curtailed by the scope of the project.

The discipline of biblical theology attempts to explain the teaching of the Bible on its own terms, using its own categories and often following the development of its themes from Genesis to Revelation. One way to view biblical theology is as a bridge between exegesis (the practice of interpreting the Bible) and systematic theology (the study of Christian doctrine and practice). With this in mind, I have attempted to focus on the teaching of Paul himself, using his own words and categories as much as possible, and showing how his teaching relates to major themes in the Bible. But I have also worked carefully through all the exegetical issues in Colossians and Philemon and have tried to think carefully through the important doctrinal and practical issues. Again, the scope of the project has necessarily limited my discussion of these issues.

Some acknowledgments: I want to thank Brian Rosner and Tom Schreiner for inviting me to contribute to this exciting new series. I especially want to thank Tom, my *Doktorvater*, who has had a great influence on my understanding of Scripture and so has had a great influence on this book. My dean and friend, Keith Plummer, helpfully suggested that I teach a graduate-level exegesis elective on Colossians and Philemon, which definitely helped the project. Thanks to the following students in that course for their sharpening effect through many enjoyable classroom discussions and through their feedback on some early drafts: Evan Carey, Justin Gambrill, Lydia Garrison, Nathan Garrison, Brandon Miller, Micah Portis, Sascha Rose, and Jon Silva. Thanks also to Caleb Daubenspeck for fielding more than a few ILL requests. Colleen McFadden, Mike Moore, and Ben O'Toole read a rough draft of the entire book, each improving it in distinct ways. Thanks to Lydia Brownback for carefully editing the manuscript. All remaining faults, of course, are my own. Finally, thanks to the Lord for giving me understanding and strength to finish this book, and thanks to friends and family for praying for me.

Kevin W. McFadden
September 15, 2022

Abbreviations

AB	Anchor Bible
ABR	*Australian Biblical Review*
Ant.	*Jewish Antiquities*, by Josephus
BDAG	*Greek-English Lexicon of the New Testament and Other Early Christian Literature*, 3rd ed.
BDF	*A Greek Grammar of the New Testament and Other Early Christian Literature*
BECNT	Baker Exegetical Commentary on the New Testament
CBR	*Currents in Biblical Research*
Diatr.	*Diatribai*, by Epictetus
Ep.	*Epistulae*, by Pliny the Younger
HBT	*Horizons in Biblical Theology*
HTR	*Harvard Theological Review*
JSNT	*Journal for the Study of the New Testament*
JTS	*Journal of Theological Studies*
LNTS	Library of New Testament Studies
NSBT	New Studies in Biblical Theology
ÖTK	Ökumenischer Taschenbuchkommentar zum Neuen Testament
PNTC	Pillar New Testament Commentaries
PRSt	*Perspectives in Religious Studies*
SNTSMS	Society for New Testament Studies Monograph Series
THGNT	Tyndale House Greek New Testament

TNTC   Tyndale New Testament Commentaries
ZECNT   Zondervan Exegetical Commentary on the New
            Testament
ZNW   *Zeitschrift für die neutestamentliche Wissenschaft und die*
            Kunde der älteren Kirche

Prologue

Hope in Difficult Circumstances

Remember my chains.
COLOSSIANS 4:18

SOMETIMES DIFFICULT EARTHLY CIRCUMSTANCES bring clarity to the heavenly hope of the gospel. Paul's letters to the Colossians and to Philemon were written in the midst of difficult circumstances: Paul was in prison, the church was in danger of false teaching, and Philemon was estranged from his slave Onesimus. But in these letters we find some of the Bible's most profound teaching about Christ and the practical difference he makes in our lives and relationships. Let us briefly, then, "remember [Paul's] chains" (Col. 4:18) by considering the difficult circumstances that led to the hopeful teaching of Colossians and Philemon.

Paul in Prison

The ministry of the gospel has never been easy. This was perhaps truest for the apostle Paul, of whom Jesus said, "I will show him how much he must suffer for the sake of my name" (Acts 9:16). Paul describes his own work as "toil" and "struggle" (Col. 1:29; 2:1), similar to how he describes the work of Epaphras, who planted the church at Colossae (4:12–13). And he uses labels for his colleagues in ministry that communicate the arduous and dangerous nature of the task: "fellow worker" (Col. 4:11; Philem. 1, 24), "fellow soldier" (Philem. 2), "fellow slave" (Col. 1:7 CSB; cf. 4:12), and "fellow prisoner" (4:10). In fact, Paul wrote these two letters from prison, most likely his two-year house arrest at Rome (c. AD 60–62; see Acts 28:16–31).[1]

Paul did not view his imprisonment as a hiatus in ministry but as a part of his ministry. We see this in Colossians 1:24–2:5, where he explains his purpose for writing. He tells the Colossians that he is suffering "for your sake, and in my flesh I am filling up what is lacking in Christ's afflictions for the sake of his body, that is, the church" (1:24). Paul does not mean that the death of Christ was insufficient to fully save. Rather, he means that the risen and ascended Christ is currently using ministers suffering "in the flesh," like Paul and Epaphras, to bring the church to full maturity (1:28; 4:12; cf. 1:22).

So the apostle continued to work in the midst of his imprisonment. He was instrumental in the conversion of Onesimus (Philem. 10). And he wrote his letter to the Colossians, which arguably contains his most profound theological reflection on the doctrine of Christ. For some scholars, the theological teaching of this letter goes so far beyond what Paul writes in his other letters that they question whether Paul could have written it.[2] I raise the issue of authorship because it affects how

---

1   This is the traditional view, and it is held by many modern scholars as well, e.g., David W. Pao, *Colossians and Philemon*, ZECNT (Grand Rapids, MI: Zondervan, 2012), 23–24. Some scholars question whether Paul could be writing from Rome because of its distance from Colossae, which is located in modern-day Turkey. Would Onesimus have traveled that far? And would Paul be planning to visit Colossae so soon after his release (Philem. 22)? Wasn't he planning to go the opposite way to Spain (see Rom. 15:23–24)? To account for this, many theorize that Paul was perhaps imprisoned at some earlier point in Ephesus, which is much closer to Colossae, and in which Paul ministered for many years; e.g., N. T. Wright, *Colossians and Philemon: An Introduction and Commentary*, TNTC (Downers Grove, IL: InterVarsity Press, 1986), 37–42. But Rome was less than a month's journey from Colossae, according to the Stanford Geospatial Network Model of the Roman World (https://orbis.stanford.edu). And we know that Paul changed his travel plans at other points (Acts 16:6–8; 2 Cor. 1:15–2:4).

2   See, e.g., Eduard Lohse, *Colossians and Philemon*, Hermeneia, trans. William R. Poehlmann and Robert J. Karris (Philadelphia: Fortress Press, 1971), 177–83. The theology of Colossians seems to be the major reason that scholars came to reject Pauline authorship

we think about the theology of Colossians. Is the teaching of this letter really from an apostle? In my view, it seems historically likely that the apostle Paul wrote and sent Colossians at the same time as Philemon because it overlaps on so many points with Philemon.[3] The profundity of its theological reflection is not a contradiction with the theology of Paul's other letters but rather an extension of his theology, sharpened by his confrontation with a false teaching that was threatening the saints in Colossae.

Colossae and the Philosophy

Colossae was a remote inland town, located in the Roman province of Asia in what is now modern-day Turkey. Paul had probably never been to Colossae when he wrote these two letters.[4] But during his third missionary journey, he spent an extended time of ministry in the large coastal city of Ephesus (c. AD 52–55; see Acts 19:1–20:1). Luke tells us that during this time "all the residents of Asia heard the word of the Lord, both Jews and Greeks" (Acts 19:10). The Colossians, along with their neighbors in Laodicea and Hierapolis, had heard the word

---

in the nineteenth and twentieth centuries until W. Bujard supported this theory with an analysis of the style of the letter (see John M. G. Barclay, *Colossians and Philemon*, T&T Clark Study Guides [New York: T&T Clark International, 1997], 20–23). Moo thinks that even today, "scholars on both sides of the debate on authorship . . . generally agree that the critical evidence in deciding the issue is the theology of the letter." Douglas J. Moo, *The Letters to the Colossians and to Philemon*, PNTC (Grand Rapids, MI: Eerdmans, 2008), 32.

3   Both letters claim to be written by Paul during an imprisonment; both mention Timothy as a cosender of the letter; both open by thanking God for the Christian virtues of faith and love; both focus on slavery (note that slavery is given much attention in the household code of Col. 3:18–4:1); both mention Onesimus the slave; both address Archippus as a minister in the church; and both send greetings from Epaphras, Mark, Aristarchus, Demas, and Luke. As Fee remarks, "It remains one of the singular mysteries in NT scholarship that so many scholars reject Pauline authorship of Colossians yet affirm the authenticity of Philemon." Gordon D. Fee, *Pauline Christology: An Exegetical-Theological Study* (Peabody, MA: Hendrickson, 2007), 289n2.

4   There is a chance that Paul could have taken the road through Colossae on his way to Ephesus at the beginning of his third missionary journey (see Acts 18:23 and 19:1). But Schnabel concludes that "since Paul did not know the Christians in Colossae and in Laodikeia personally (cf. Col 2:1), it is rather likely that he did not travel to Ephesus through the Lykos Valley and the Maeander Valley in A.D. 52." Eckhard J. Schnabel, *Early Christian Mission* (Downers Grove, IL: InterVarsity Press, 2004), 1200.

from Epaphras (Col. 1:7; 4:13). So Epaphras was probably one of Paul's converts in Ephesus, which was about a week's journey on foot from Colossae. One can imagine Epaphras hearing the gospel and then traveling home up the eastern road that led along the Maeander River until it turned slightly south into the Lycus River Valley and eventually to Colossae. Once there, he told his friends and family the gospel, and they received Christ Jesus as their Lord (2:6).[5]

But soon after, the Colossian believers were confronted with a false teaching. Paul apparently caught wind of this through Epaphras, who was with Paul in his imprisonment (Philem. 23). So he decided to write to these believers "in order that no one may delude [them] with plausible arguments" (Col. 2:4). He warns, "See to it that no one takes you captive by philosophy and empty deceit" (2:8). More literally, Paul writes in this verse of "*the* philosophy [*tēs philosophias*]," likely referring to a specific teaching. Perhaps the false teachers labeled their teaching as "philosophy" in order to gain credibility, just as someone today might label their view "scientific." But what was the philosophy? It is most clearly explained in the polemical section of Colossians 2:16–23, where we see that it required law-keeping and angelic visions to reach the fullness of salvation.

The false teachers were ready to "pass judgment" on the Colossian saints unless they followed certain food restrictions and kept certain holidays (2:16; cf. 2:21). Most likely they were teaching that believers must keep the food and calendar requirements of the Mosaic law in order to be saved. The law prohibits eating unclean animals and touching their carcasses (Lev. 11), drinking from unclean vessels (Lev. 11:34), and drinking wine for priests in the tent of meeting and for those under a Nazirite vow (Lev. 10:9; Num. 6:3). After the exile to Babylon, some Jews living in pagan cultures would refrain from all meat and wine in order to avoid defilement (Dan. 1:8–16). And we know that after the

---

5   Some copies of Col. 1:7 say Epaphras "is a faithful minister of Christ on *our* behalf" (NIV) rather than "on *your* behalf" (ESV). This wording would imply that Paul sent Epaphras to Colossae. But unfortunately it is very difficult to decide which wording was original to Paul's letter.

exile, there was a Jewish presence in Colossae because Josephus tells us that two thousand Jewish families had been moved from Babylon to Phrygia, the ancient name for the region of Colossae.[6] Regarding the holiday requirements, the law regulated Israel's yearly, monthly, and weekly calendar (Lev. 25). And Paul's threefold description, "festival," "new moon," and "Sabbath" (Col. 2:16), is found several times in the Old Testament with reference to the calendar regulations of the law (e.g., 2 Chron. 2:4). Finally, Paul says that the calendar and food regulations "are a shadow of the things to come" (Col. 2:17), using typological reasoning like the author of Hebrews, who wrote, "The law has but a shadow of the good things to come" (Heb. 10:1). The philosophy, therefore, probably taught that believers must keep the Mosaic calendar and food laws in order to be saved. Perhaps it also taught that Gentile believers must be circumcised according to the law (cf. Col. 2:11).

For this reason, a few scholars have argued that Colossians confronts the same issue Paul confronted in Galatians, where Jewish-Christian teachers were compelling Gentile Christians to be circumcised and keep the Jewish law.[7] But most have rightly observed that the issue in Colossae was different and more complex. The false teachers were apparently promoting law-keeping as an ascetic practice that would lead to heavenly, angelic visions: "Let no one disqualify you, insisting on asceticism and worship of angels, going on in detail about visions, puffed up without reason by his sensuous mind" (Col. 2:18; cf. 2:23). So the false teachers were ready to "disqualify" from salvation anyone who did not share in these ascetic practices and angelic visions. But what were these visions? This aspect of the philosophy is very difficult to understand because Paul does not give much explanation and because Colossians 2:18, the main piece of evidence, is difficult to translate.

Today there are two basic views. Some scholars suggest that the philosophy was a kind of Jewish mysticism. In this view the "worship of angels" in Colossians 2:18 refers to the angelic worship of God, like we

---

6 Josephus, *Ant.* 12.3.4.
7 See especially Wright, *Colossians*, 26–33, 109.

see in Revelation 4–5 and other Jewish apocalypses. "Going on in detail" is more literally translated "entering," and perhaps it refers to someone's entrance into heaven to see and join with the angels in their worship.[8] Other scholars think that the philosophy was syncretistic, drawing on aspects of Judaism but also aspects of paganism. In this view, "worship of angels" in Colossians 2:18 refers to the human worship or veneration of angels. Arnold has documented how common it was in local folk religion for people to call upon angels for help, even Jewish people.[9] A fourth-century Christian council in the nearby city of Laodicea had to forbid Christians from worshiping angels and clergy from becoming magicians or astrologers.[10] If the philosophy was syncretistic, then perhaps "entering" refers to initiation into the visionary experiences of one of the pagan mystery religions, as it does in inscriptions at a pagan temple at Claros, north of Ephesus.[11]

A choice between these two views is difficult. I am inclined toward the syncretistic view (the second view) because a pagan fear of angelic powers seems to fit the emphasis in Colossians on the lordship of Christ over all demonic powers (1:16; 2:8, 10, 15, 18–19, 20). Perhaps the Colossians were afraid of "missing out" on something by simply holding to Christ. They were being told they needed do something else or have other religious experiences or call upon angels to help them in their daily lives. This situation may sound worlds away to a modern reader. But Thurston observes that "Colossians addresses the perennial centrality of Jesus Christ, who in this letter is the standard against which all else is measured. This Christocentricity was asserted in a world of cultural, philosophic, and religious pluralism not unlike our own."[12]

---

8   For a classic and influential argument for this position, see the two chapters by Fred O. Francis, in *Conflict at Colossae: A Problem in the Interpretation of Early Christianity Illustrated by Selected Modern Studies*, rev. ed., ed. Fred O. Francis and Wayne A. Meeks (Missoula, MT: SBL and Scholars, 1975), 163–207.

9   Clinton E. Arnold, *The Colossian Syncretism: The Interface between Christianity and Folk Belief at Colossae* (Grand Rapids, MI: Baker, 1996), 11–89.

10   Arnold, *Colossian Syncretism*, 86.

11   See Arnold, *Colossian Syncretism*, 104–7, 127–31, 155–57.

12   Bonnie Bowman Thurston, *All the Fullness of God: The Christ of Colossians* (Eugene, OR: Cascade, 2017), viii.

In a complex, pluralistic world, Christians can be afraid that they are missing out on something. And we are often told that we are. But Paul writes to teach us that we are not. Christ is sufficient for everything in our lives, even the mundane but difficult relational conflict between Philemon and his slave Onesimus.

Philemon and Onesimus

The circumstance in Paul's letter to Philemon that probably seems most difficult for modern readers is the fact that Onesimus was enslaved. Pauline scholarship has gone back and forth about how we should compare ancient slavery in the Roman world and modern slavery in America. Some have argued that ancient slavery was not as bad as modern slavery, and others have argued that it was terrible. The truth is probably somewhere in the middle and varied in experience for different people.[13]

Nevertheless, it is important for modern readers of Philemon to see that the main offender in this particular situation seems to have been the slave Onesimus (Philem. 11, 18). This can be hard for us to imagine, because those who live in a liberal democracy can sometimes think of no greater evil than taking someone's liberty. Paul's letter to Philemon does have something to say to the modern issue of slavery.[14] But Onesimus's enslavement is not the main problem in the letter. The main problem is the estrangement and hostility between Onesimus and Philemon, which can be seen from Paul's main point in the letter: "So if you consider me your partner, receive him as you would receive me" (17).

What had led to this estrangement? Reconstructing the historical situation is very difficult because of the delicate, pastoral way Paul speaks of it. Traditionally, interpreters have assumed that Onesimus was a fugitive slave who ran away from his master Philemon

---

13 For an overview of scholarship on Paul and slavery that has influenced this paragraph, see John Byron, "Paul and the Background of Slavery: The *Status Quaestionis* in New Testament Scholarship," *CBR* 3.1 (2004): 116–49.

14 I address the issue of slavery on pp. 83–85, 95–97.

and perhaps stole property.[15] This would explain why Onesimus was parted from Philemon (15) as well as Paul's allusive references to his uselessness (11) and his having wronged Philemon (18). Lampe, however, has argued that Onesimus was not a fugitive slave who just happened to run into Paul; rather, he purposely went to Paul to intercede for a previous altercation between Philemon and Onesimus.[16] This would better explain how Onesimus met Paul, especially if Paul was imprisoned in Rome, a city of over a million people. Comparison is often made with a letter of Pliny the Younger, to whom a freedman went in order to intercede between him and his former master for whom he still worked.[17] A problem with this view is that there is no indication that Onesimus was in danger of experiencing Philemon's anger and punishment, unlike the texts appealed to by Lampe and Pliny's letter that repeatedly mentions the master's anger. Rather, the issues raised in this letter are the "useless" conduct of Onesimus and the suggestion that he has perhaps wronged Philemon. These issues are best explained by his having run away.[18]

From the delicate way Paul writes, it is clear that it would not be easy for Philemon to welcome back his estranged slave. Neither could it have been easy for Onesimus to return to his master. But in this letter we see a powerful example of how the hope of the gospel makes a difference in believers' relationships with one another both now and forever (15).

---

15   Mitchell shows that the fugitive slave view was held by Athanasius, Basil of Caesarea, Chrysostom, Jerome, and others. Margaret M. Mitchell, "John Chrysostom on Philemon: A Second Look," *HTR* 88.1 (1995): 145–47.

16   Peter Lampe, "Keine 'Sklavenflucht' des Onesimus," *ZNW* 76 (1985): 135–37.

17   Pliny the Younger, *Ep.* 9.21. For an accessible translation, see N. T. Wright, *Paul and the Faithfulness of God* (Minneapolis: Fortress Press, 2013), 3.

18   Another theory is that Philemon had sent Onesimus to help Paul, argued most recently by Stephen E. Young, *Our Brother Beloved: Purpose and Community in Paul's Letter to Philemon* (Waco, TX: Baylor University Press, 2021). In my view, Young unconvincingly downplays Onesimus's wrongdoing in Philem. 11 and 18 in order to save the letter from the traditional reading, which he thinks is inherently oppressive (*Our Brother Beloved*, 7–38). I agree that the traditional theory has been applied oppressively in America's past, but this misapplication does not invalidate the theory.

Hidden with Christ in God

These difficult earthly circumstances led Paul to reflect and write more deeply about the heavenly hope of the gospel. The main points of these two letters are essentially practical: walk in Christ (Col. 2:6) and welcome your brother (Philem. 17). But these practical instructions are rooted in the deep theology of the letters, especially their Christology.

Many have observed the emphasis on Christology in Paul's letter to the Colossians.[19] If the New Testament is the Rocky Mountains of Christology, then Colossians is its Pikes Peak. Prominent vistas include the famous poem about Christ (1:15–20), the statement that Christ is the one "in whom are hidden all the treasures of wisdom and knowledge" (2:3), and Paul's summary and application of his Christology for baptized believers in Colossians 3:1–4.

In this book, I explore the Christology of Colossians in four chapters that roughly follow the argument of the letter (although they are not based on its four chapters). Chapter 1 introduces Christ as our hidden hope. Chapter 2 dives deeper into Paul's teaching about the preeminence of the Son. Chapter 3 spells out the sufficiency of Christ by examining Paul's teaching about our new life in Christ above. And chapter 4 builds upon this indicative reality by working through Paul's imperatives to live out the new life below. Finally, chapter 5 summarizes the theology of Philemon, demonstrating how the hidden hope of Christ was sufficient for the difficult situation facing Philemon and Onesimus.

In Colossians and Philemon, Paul roots his practical appeals in a rich theology of Christ. He teaches that our hope in the midst of difficult circumstances is the preeminent and sufficient Christ. This hope is hidden in heaven above and not yet openly revealed below. Therefore, the main theme of this book is that the preeminent and sufficient Christ is our hidden hope.

---

19 For example, Barclay observes that "the Christology of Colossians is as confident and broad in scope as is to be found anywhere in the New Testament." John M. G. Barclay, "Ordinary but Different: Colossians and Hidden Moral Identity," *ABR* 49 (2001): 36.

1

Christ, Our Hope

Christ in you, the hope of glory.

COLOSSIANS 1:27

THIS CHAPTER INTRODUCES the hope of the gospel, which is Christ himself. We begin where Paul begins. In the midst of his imprisonment and the threat of false teaching at Colossae, the apostle begins with thanksgiving. He is grateful to God the Father for the fruit he is bearing in the lives of the Colossians: their faith in Christ and love for all the saints because of the hope of the gospel of his beloved Son.

Thanksgiving

Colossians opens with a prayer of thanksgiving (1:3–4), like most of Paul's letters. But this was no mere formality. Prayer and thanksgiving were Paul's regular discipline: "We *always* thank God, the Father of our Lord Jesus Christ, when we pray for you" (1:3); "We have not ceased to pray for you" (1:9).[1] Epaphras, the evangelist of Colossae, had this discipline as well: "Epaphras . . . greets you, always struggling on your behalf in his prayers" (4:12). And Paul instructs the Colossians

---

1 Perhaps Paul set aside times to pray in the morning, noon, and evening, like Daniel: "He got down on his knees three times a day and prayed and gave thanks before his God" (Dan. 6:10).

to pursue the same discipline: "Continue steadfastly in prayer, being watchful in it with thanksgiving" (4:2).

Thanksgiving is the appropriate human response to "the grace of God," as Paul describes the gospel in Colossians 1:6. God's grace leads to our gratitude. In Colossians Paul uses the Greek word *charis* to refer both to the grace of God (e.g., 1:2 and 4:18) and to our response of "thankfulness" (3:16). He also uses the similar words *eucharistos* and *eucharisteō* to speak of our thankfulness: "And be thankful [*eucharistoi*]" (3:15); "giving thanks [*eucharistountes*] to the Father" (1:12); "giving thanks [*eucharistountes*] to God the Father through him" (3:17).

Thanksgiving is closely related to the purpose of this letter. Whereas the false teachers were telling the Colossians to look beyond Christ, Paul calls them to be thankful for the redemption God has already given them in Christ (1:12; 2:6–7).[2] In Colossians 3:15–17 he associates calls for thankfulness with the peace of Christ, with the word of Christ, and with the name of Christ. Pao observes that "the call to thanksgiving as a response is the call to live in light of the sovereignty of God and his Son," concluding that "it is precisely Paul's emphasis on the supremacy and sufficiency of Christ that prompted him to focus on the life of thanksgiving."[3]

Finally, it is notable that thanksgiving is consistently directed toward God the Father in Colossians (1:3, 12; 3:17), for the Father is the ultimate source of all grace. Colossians 1:1–14, in fact, emphasizes the Father's role in our redemption. Many have observed that the greeting of Colossians is unique among Paul's letters in that it only mentions "our Father" and not the Lord Jesus Christ (1:2). Moo's comment seems on point: "Perhaps, in a letter that elevates Christ, Paul wants at the outset to anchor the person of Christ firmly to God the Father."[4] The preeminence and sufficiency of Christ does not eclipse the glory of the Father. Instead, the

---

2   For this point, I am indebted to Michael Wolter, *Der Brief an die Kolosser, Der Brief an Philemon*, ÖTK 12 (Gütersloh, Germany: Gerd Mohn, 1993), 64.

3   David W. Pao, *Thanksgiving: An Investigation of a Pauline Theme*, NSBT 13 (Downers Grove, IL: InterVarsity Press, 2002), 114, 116.

4   Douglas J. Moo, *The Letters to the Colossians and to Philemon*, PNTC (Grand Rapids, MI: Eerdmans, 2008), 83.

gospel teaches that *the Father* has brought about redemption *through* "his beloved Son" (1:13).[5] Thus the Father is the ultimate source of the grace of redemption and the one who deserves all our thanksgiving.

Beale concludes with these helpful words of application:

> When there is no prayerful contemplation of divine blessings, there can be no attitude of thanksgiving. . . . Continual reflection on the Giver of good gifts causes us to be more conscious of and thankful for those gifts. . . . Christians impoverish themselves when they do not prayerfully consider how they have experienced God's grace, and this theological impoverishment results in an unthankful attitude. To the extent that one has a prayerful attitude, to that extent one will have an attitude of thanksgiving.[6]

Paul clearly had such an attitude of prayerful contemplation. As he remembered the Colossians from prison, he was filled with joy (1:24; 2:5), and he was thankful for the faith and love the Father had worked in them.

Faith and Love

Paul first thanks God for the Colossians' "faith in Christ Jesus" (1:4), probably because faith is the first step of the Christian life. Their faith had come by hearing: Paul says they had heard the gospel, understood it, and learned it from Epaphras (1:5–7; cf. 1:23). And they had come to believe it—that is, they had come to believe in Christ himself (1:4; 2:5). Colossians 2:6, the verse that states the main point of the letter, also mentions their coming to faith, when they had "received Christ Jesus the Lord." Here we see that faith is a receiving of Christ as Lord, expressed in the confession that "Jesus is Lord" (cf. Rom. 10:9; 1 Cor. 12:3).[7]

---

5 "His beloved Son" in Col. 1:13 likely alludes to the Father's pronouncement at Jesus's baptism and transfiguration (see Mark 1:11; 9:7 and parallels).

6 G. K. Beale, *Colossians and Philemon*, BECNT (Grand Rapids, MI: Baker Academic, 2019), 383–84. Note that these words are a conclusion from the opening thanksgiving of Philemon, which is very similar to the one in Colossians.

7 Perhaps Paul also refers to their faith in Christ in Col. 1:2. Most modern English versions translate the verse similarly to the ESV: "To the saints and faithful brothers in Christ

Faith in Christ is not only the first step in the Christian life but the continuing walk of the Christian life. Here we come to the main point of Colossians: "Therefore, as you received Christ Jesus the Lord, *so walk in him*, rooted and built up in him and established in the faith, just as you were taught, abounding in thanksgiving" (Col. 2:6–7). The Colossians must continue to walk by faith (cf. 2 Cor. 5:7). Indeed, they will only be presented as "holy and blameless and above reproach" at the final judgment *if* they continue in the faith (Col. 1:22–23). That is, they will only be finally saved if they continue in the faith. In Colossians 1:23 and 2:7 Paul describes continuing to believe in Christ with the language of architecture and agriculture: "stable and steadfast"; "rooted and built up in him and established in the faith." His point is that Christ must be the soil in which believers grow and the foundation on whom believers are constructed.[8] Believers must not shift away from the hope of the gospel they heard (1:23); they must continue to walk in Christ.

Second, Paul thanks God because he had heard of the love that they had for all the saints (1:4). The Colossians' common faith in Christ had created a new family. They were now brothers and sisters (1:1, 2; 4:7, 9, 15) and "beloved" to one another (1:7; 4:9, 14). Their love for "*all* the saints" may refer to their love for fellow believers in the neighboring towns of Laodicea and Hierapolis (cf. 4:13–16). Perhaps Paul was also thinking of their love for him, made known to him by Epaphras (1:8). One of the goals of Paul's ministry was that believers in every place would be "knit together in love" (2:2; cf. 2:19). He says later in the letter that love is the crowning virtue that "binds [everyone] together in perfect harmony" (3:14).[9] It makes sense, then, that when he heard

---

at Colossae." But as a statement of Christian identity it makes more sense to see Paul speaking about their faith rather than their faithfulness. So perhaps we should follow the older translations of Tyndale and Luther: "brethren that believe in Christ"; "*den gläubigen Brüdern in Christo*." So Eduard Lohse, *Colossians and Philemon*, Hermeneia, trans. William R. Poehlmann and Robert J. Karris (Philadelphia: Fortress, 1971), 9.

8 In Col. 1:23 and 2:7, perhaps the passive voice of the participles "stable" (lit. "founded"), "rooted," "built up," and "established" implies that God the Father is the one who does this work through Christ. So Moo, *Colossians and Philemon*, 181.

9 I have changed the ESV's "everything" to "everyone." For my reasoning, see p. 78n12.

about the Colossians' love in the midst of his imprisonment, he was filled with joy and thanksgiving to God.

One of the few references to the Holy Spirit in this letter describes him as the agent of the Colossians' love (1:8). Perhaps Paul does not mention the Spirit often in Colossians because he focuses on the supremacy and sufficiency of Christ. Nevertheless, he does say that the Spirit is the agent of divine revelation, praying to God that the Colossians "may be filled with the knowledge of his will in all *spiritual* wisdom and understanding" (1:9). The Spirit is also the agent of the composition or performance of Christian music, for Paul instructs the Colossians to "let the word of Christ dwell in you richly . . . singing psalms and hymns and *spiritual* songs" (3:16). And he was the agent of the Colossians' love, for Epaphras had made known to Paul their love "[by] the Spirit" (1:8).[10] We would not be wrong to say that the Spirit was also the agent of their faith, for Paul says elsewhere that "no one can say, 'Jesus is Lord,' except by the Holy Spirit" (1 Cor. 12:3 CSB).

Finally, the faith and love of the Colossians were rooted in their heavenly hope: "because of the hope laid up for you in heaven."[11] They had heard about this hope from Epaphras "in the word of the truth, the gospel" (Col. 1:5). Thus, the foundation of their faith in Christ, their love for the saints, and Paul's thanksgiving to God was the hope of the gospel.

The Hope of the Gospel

What is the hope of the gospel according to Colossians? In a word, it is Christ. Paul tells the Colossians that "the hope of glory" is "Christ in you" (1:27). Those who have Christ dwelling in them (by his Spirit) have the hope that they will one day share in the glory of his resurrection (cf. Rom. 5–8). Hope is by definition oriented toward this unseen future

---

10 I have changed the ESV's "in the Spirit" to "by the Spirit" because the preposition *en* is most likely instrumental. So Murray J. Harris, *Colossians and Philemon*, vol. 12, Exegetical Guide to the Greek New Testament (Grand Rapids, MI: Eerdmans, 1991), 23.

11 Paul was apparently the first to associate the three theological virtues of faith, hope, and love (Wolter, *Kolosser*, 51). Cf. 1 Cor. 13:13; 1 Thess. 1:3; 5:8.

reality, "for who hopes for what he sees?" (Rom. 8:24). But the hope of the resurrection is also rooted in the past reality of the cross of Christ through which the Father has accomplished our redemption and reconciliation.

Redemption in Christ

In his opening prayer, Paul reminds the Colossians that the Father has accomplished redemption in his beloved Son (Col. 1:14). While *redemption* can be used to describe salvation generally, here it specifically refers to a payment for our release from captivity.[12] Paul's reasoning is fleshed out in Ephesians, a letter probably written at the same time, in which he says that this payment is the cross: "In him we have redemption through his blood, the forgiveness of our trespasses, according to the riches of his grace" (Eph. 1:7).

What was the captivity from which Christ's blood redeemed us? Paul defines this redemption as "the forgiveness of sins" (Col. 1:14). So the cross has redeemed us from the captivity of the debt of our sins against God. And as a result we are also freed from captivity to "the domain of darkness" (1:13) or the evil kingdom of Satan. Satan has authority over fallen humanity because of his role in our sins: he tempts us to sin as he did with Eve (Gen. 3:1–5), and he accuses us of sin as he did with Job (Job 1:6–12). People today tend to reject or forget about Satan and demonic powers, but the Colossians were acutely aware of the presence of angels and demons. Perhaps the philosophy promised them deliverance from the threat of demonic powers. But Paul reminds them that the Father had already delivered them "from the domain of darkness" (Col. 1:13), because he had forgiven their sins in Christ (1:14).

He has also "transferred us to the kingdom of his beloved Son" (1:13). In Christ, believers are bona fide citizens and heirs of the kingdom of God, for the Father has qualified us "to share in the inheritance of the saints in light" (1:12).[13] The redeemed, then, are rightly called "saints"

---

12 This conclusion has been influenced by Leon Morris, *The Apostolic Preaching of the Cross*, 3rd ed. (Grand Rapids, MI: Eerdmans, 1965), 16–18.

13 Some commentators argue that "saints in light" in Col. 1:12 refers to angels, drawing parallels with Qumran texts that describe angels as God's "holy ones" (e.g., Lohse, *Colossians*

or God's "holy people" now, in the present (1:2, 4, 12, 26). And we also have hope for the future that at the final judgment he will "present [us] holy and blameless and above reproach before him" (1:22), provided of course that we continue in the faith (1:23).[14]

Reconciliation through Christ

In the famous poem about Christ in Colossians 1:15–20, Paul teaches that the Father has also accomplished reconciliation through the cross of Christ. The word "reconcile" implies the problem of rebellion. Although God created all things through and for his Son (1:16), these things are now at war with him. Yet through the incarnate Son he has reconciled "all things, whether on earth or in heaven, making peace by the blood of his cross" (1:20).

Interpreters and theologians struggle to explain Colossians 1:20. Does this verse teach universal salvation for all people on earth and angels in heaven? This view seems unlikely when one considers what Paul says in the next paragraph about the need for people to continue in the faith to stand blameless before God (1:21–23) and what he says later in the letter about God's coming wrath against disobedient people (3:5) and Christ's triumph over evil angels (2:15). Arnold observes that the language Paul uses in Colossians 2:15 "leaves no room for a reconciliation as friends."[15] Instead, we must see that reconciliation in Colossians 1:20 is a category broader than salvation. It refers to the universal peace God has brought about through the cross. The war has ended! Some enemies have been "disarmed" and brought into submission (2:15). Other enemies have been turned into friends.

---

and Philemon, 36). But in the context of Col. 1:2, 4, and 26 it makes more sense to see a consistent reference to God's holy people.

14 Many interpreters detect exodus imagery and typology in Paul's teaching about redemption in Col. 1:12–14. Just as the Lord delivered Israel from captivity and brought them into their inheritance, so he has now redeemed believers to bring us into our inheritance. See the extensive discussion of Beale in *Colossians and Philemon*, 72–74.

15 Clinton E. Arnold, *The Colossian Syncretism: The Interface between Christianity and Folk Belief at Colossae* (Grand Rapids, MI: Baker, 1996), 268.

Paul goes on to say the Colossians are in the latter category: "And you, who once were alienated and hostile in mind, doing evil deeds, he has now reconciled in his body of flesh by his death, in order to present you holy and blameless and above reproach before him" (1:21–22). The Father is indeed our source of peace (1:2). And his work of reconciliation through the death of his Son is the foundation of our future and final hope.

Our Hidden Hope

Thus the hope of the gospel is Christ. The Father has accomplished our redemption and reconciliation through his Son in order to present us blameless at the final judgment. When he appears, we will appear with him in the glory of his resurrection (3:4). But until that day he remains hidden in heaven at the right hand of God (3:1), and our lives are hidden with him as well (3:3). The Christological content of the gospel, then, is rightly described as "the hope laid up for you in heaven" (1:5). Further, this description introduces us to the "heavenly eschatology" that characterizes Colossians, for it contains both eschatological ("the hope") and heavenly ("in heaven") categories.

The gospel of Christ is eschatological in that it is a message about the eschaton, the end of time when God will establish his kingdom, judge his enemies, and redeem his people through the Messiah. On the one hand, Paul teaches that this kingdom has come already with Christ (1:12–14; cf. 4:11). The Father has defeated his enemies and redeemed his people through the cross of Christ. This inaugurated aspect of eschatology is emphasized in Colossians. On the other hand, Paul teaches in Colossians that Christ has not yet appeared (3:4). We look forward in hope to share in the glory of his resurrection (3:4) and the inheritance of the saints (1:12).

This "already but not yet" eschatology overlaps with Paul's heavenly categories in Colossians. Christ is already reigning at the right hand of God in heaven, but his lordship is not yet openly revealed on the earth (3:1–4).[16]

---

16 Beker helpfully speaks of "the present but hidden lordship of Christ." J. Christiaan Beker, *Paul the Apostle: The Triumph of God in Life and Thought* (Philadelphia: Fortress, 1980), 19.

According to Colossians, then, the hope of the gospel is hidden in heaven. And thus the main theme of this book is that Christ is our hidden hope.

Bearing Fruit and Increasing

The hidden nature of the gospel, however, does not mean that it has nothing to do with the here and now. For Paul tells the Colossians that "in the whole world [the gospel] is bearing fruit and increasing—as it also does among you, since the day you heard it and understood the grace of God in truth" (1:6).[17]

Externally, the gospel was increasing and spreading around the entire world. Writing in the early AD 60s, Paul says Christ had been "proclaimed in all creation under heaven" (1:23). He was revealed not only to the Jews but to the Gentile nations (1:27). And Paul was offering him freely to every person: "Him we proclaim, warning *everyone* and teaching *everyone* with all wisdom, that we may present *everyone* mature in Christ" (1:28). The point is that the gospel is not an esoteric message offering salvation to a limited "in group." The philosophy attempted to disqualify anyone who did not keep their regulations or experience their visions (2:16–23). But the true gospel is offered openly to everyone so that it may be believed by everyone in the world. Regarding the phrase "in the whole world" in Colossians 1:6, Lightfoot insightfully comments:

> More lurks under these words than appears on the surface. The true Gospel, the Apostle seems to say, proclaims its truth by its universality. The false gospels are outgrowths of local circumstances, of special idiosyncrasies; the true gospel is the same everywhere. The false gospels address themselves to limited circles; the true Gospel proclaims itself boldly throughout the world. Heresies are at best ethnic: truth is essentially catholic.[18]

17 Many commentators suggest that Paul's language about "bearing fruit and increasing" (Col. 1:6, 10) alludes to the command to "be fruitful and multiply" in Gen. 1:28 (see especially Beale, *Colossians and Philemon*, 42, 48–50, 59). But this allusion is not clear to me because of the difference in wording and meaning of the two contexts.

18 J. B. Lightfoot, *St. Paul's Epistles to the Colossians and to Philemon* (Lynn, MA: Hendrickson, 1982), 134–35.

This catholic nature of the true gospel is a correlate of the universal lordship of Christ. He is the true Lord of the whole world, even though he is currently hidden above.

Internally, the gospel was also bearing the fruit of faith and love among the Colossians. And Paul prays that they would bear fruit even more: "And so, from the day we heard, we have not ceased to pray for you, asking that you may be filled with the knowledge of his will in all spiritual wisdom and understanding, so as to walk in a manner worthy of the Lord, fully pleasing to him, bearing fruit in every good work and increasing in the knowledge of God" (1:9–10). In contrast with the "wisdom" of the philosophy, Paul prays that they would be filled with the knowledge of *God's* will (1:9). Moo rightly comments that "what Paul has in mind is not some particular or special direction for one's life (as we often use the phrase 'God's will'), but a deep and abiding understanding of the revelation of Christ and all that he means for the universe (vv. 15–20) and for the Colossians (vv. 21–23)."[19] As a result, they will "walk in a manner worthy of the Lord, fully pleasing to him" (1:10).

This reference to the Colossians' "walk" anticipates the heart of the letter: "As you received Christ Jesus the Lord, so walk in him" (2:6). *Walking* in Colossians refers both to walking by faith in Christ (cf. 2 Cor. 5:7) as well as walking in "every good work" that pleases Christ (cf. Col. 3:7; 4:5).[20] And it is interesting that the Christian walk is bookended by theological knowledge in Paul's prayer in 1:9–10. Walking in Christ is both rooted in the knowledge of God's will and followed by a deeper knowledge of God.

Paul finishes his prayer with a request for divinely enabled perseverance, that they would be "strengthened with all power, according to his glorious might, for all endurance and patience with joy" (1:11). Growth in the gospel is never complete here and now, because we are still waiting for the hidden Christ to be revealed. Our great need in

---

19 Moo, *Colossians and Philemon*, 93.
20 *Pace* Wright, who sees the emphasis only on ethical conduct in Col. 2:6 (*Colossians and Philemon*, 104).

the meantime is "endurance and patience with joy." Thankfully, it is the glorious power of God himself who produces this fruit of perseverance in us.[21] This is another reason for hope. God's kingdom can seem as small as a mustard seed, especially in a small town like Colossae. But the hidden hope of the gospel was bearing fruit and increasing in them and in the whole world.

Conclusion

Paul's letter to the Colossians opens with thanksgiving to God the Father for the fruit he had borne in the Colossians: faith in Christ Jesus and love for all the saints. Their faith and love were rooted in the hope of the gospel they had heard from Epaphras: Christ himself! The Father has redeemed and reconciled us through his beloved Son in order to present us as holy before him at the final judgment. Until that day Christ, our hope, remains hidden in heaven above. Yet his gospel is bearing fruit and growing throughout the world below. In the next chapter we dive deeper into Paul's teaching about the Son.

---

21 Arnold observes in Col. 1:11 the "extraordinary emphasis on the divine power ('being empowered with power by power!')" (Arnold, *Colossian Syncretism*, 303). Cf. Paul's own reliance on divine power in his mission: "For this I toil, struggling with all his energy that he powerfully works within me" (Col. 1:29).

Christ, God's Son

The Son is the image of the invisible God.
COLOSSIANS 1:15 NIV

IN THIS CHAPTER WE LEARN that the Father's beloved Son is preeminent in everything. The Colossians were in danger of being deceived to think they must look beyond Christ to find deeper or higher wisdom. But Paul labors to convince them that they need not and cannot find anything beyond Christ, for the Son is the revelation of God, the image of God, the fullness of God, and the wisdom of God. He is our preeminent hope.

The Revelation of God

We first rediscover an idea almost lost in the modern world: revelation. God has revealed himself in Christ. Four times in Colossians Paul speaks of the gospel as a "mystery" that God has "revealed" (1:26, 27; 2:2; 4:3). In biblical theology, the word *mystery* refers to something that was hidden previously but is now revealed. For example, when the prophet Daniel explains the meaning of King Nebuchadnezzar's dream, the king responds, "Truly, your God is God of gods and Lord of kings, and a revealer of mysteries, for you have been able to reveal this mystery" (Dan. 2:47). Paul uses the word in a similar way when he calls the word of God a "mystery hidden for ages and generations but now revealed to his saints" (Col. 1:26). There is a sense in which the gospel was revealed beforehand, for Paul sees it as something prophesied in the Old Testament.[1] But the emphasis in Colossians is on the hiddenness of the gospel before the coming of Christ. Christ has "now" been revealed in a way that he was not previously known.

How has he been revealed? In Colossians 1:24–2:5, the passage that most clearly explains the mystery, Paul says that Christ is revealed through his own preaching. As he proclaims Christ, the mystery is being revealed among the nations. Similarly, Paul later asks the Colossians to pray for an open door for him to declare the mystery "so that I may reveal it" (4:4 CSB). In answer to our question, then, Christ is revealed through the apostolic proclamation of the gospel. This gospel was entrusted to other faithful ministers like Epaphras (1:7), and it is written down for us in the pages of the New Testament.

The fundamental revelation of the gospel is the saving knowledge of Christ. Paul speaks of "this mystery, which is Christ in you" (1:27), "God's mystery, which is Christ" (2:2),[2] and "the mystery of Christ" (4:3). This phrase probably means "the mystery that is Christ" in light of Colossians 1:27.[3] So as the gospel is proclaimed, Christ is revealed. On the one hand, he is revealed to the whole world, for Paul was tasked to proclaim him to everyone (1:28). On the other hand, he has been particularly revealed to the saints (1:26–27), for Paul says that the mystery is not only "Christ" but "Christ *in you*" (1:27; cf. Gal. 2:20). He is revealed in the experience of his indwelling presence or in the saving knowledge of Christ. He is revealed when someone comes to believe the gospel or to "under[stand] the grace of God in truth" (Col. 1:6). Barclay observes that "if in Romans faith is characterized by obedience,

---

1   Note the prophetic texts about Christ to which Paul alludes in Col. 1:15 and 18 (Ps. 89:27) and in Col. 3:1 (Ps. 110:1).

2   The phrase "God's mystery, which is Christ" (Col. 2:2) is one of the most difficult textual variants in the letter. It is possible that the correct reading is "the mystery of God the Father of Christ" (so, e.g., THGNT).

3   In other words, it is an epexegetical genitive; so Murray J. Harris, *Colossians and Philemon* (Grand Rapids, MI: Eerdmans, 1991), 194.

here it is most closely associated with 'knowledge' (1:6, 9, 10, 27; 2:2, 3; 3:10), 'wisdom' (1:8, 28; 2:3, 23; 3:16; 4:5) and 'understanding' (1:9; 2:2)."[4] The Colossians had come to believe in Christ because God had revealed Christ to them.

And Paul writes this letter to help them understand the immense value of this revelation. In Colossians 1:24–2:5 he recounts his suffering, toil, and struggle in order to explain his purpose for writing: that they would not be wooed away from their faith in Christ (2:4–5). The Colossians must remember Paul's chains (4:18) not only so they can pray for him but to recall that he is suffering for their sake (1:24). Why would Paul continue to proclaim Christ to the point of imprisonment? Because of the immense value of Christ for those who believe. To have Christ is to possess all "riches" (1:27; 2:2). We are not poor if we know Christ. The riches of the universe are not found in law-keeping or visionary insight. They are revealed by God as we hear the gospel of Christ, believe in Christ, and experience the indwelling presence of Christ. And all this is only a down payment of glorious riches to come at the resurrection, for "Christ in you" is "the hope of glory" (1:27). The second coming of Christ in fact is the culminating revelation of God. It is the day when Christ "is *revealed*" and believers "will be *revealed* with him in glory" (Col. 3:4 CSB).[5]

In the next two sections, we approach the holy ground of divine revelation: the poem about Christ in Colossians 1:15–20. It appears without fanfare on the tail of Paul's opening thanksgiving and prayer. But soon we realize we are standing in the holy of holies of Colossians. This passage is often called the "Christ hymn" because many scholars think Paul is quoting a preexisting song sung in the worship of Christ. While this origin theory is speculative, the poetic character of Colossians 1:15–20 is evident to all because of the parallelism between the

---

4   John M. G. Barclay, "Ordinary but Different: Colossians and Hidden Moral Identity," *ABR* 49 (2001): 35–36.

5   The verb translated "appear" by the ESV in Col. 3:4 (*phaneroō*) is the same word translated "reveal" in Col. 1:26 (cf. *phaneroō* in Col. 4:4). In Col. 3:4, the verbs are passive, probably assuming that God is the agent of this final revelation.

first and second half of the passage and the repetition of certain key words and phrases.[6] Hengel observes that in the poetry of the New Testament we see its boldest Christological claims.[7] That is certainly the case here, for here Paul claims that the beloved Son of God is pre-eminent in everything because he is the image and fullness of God.

The Image of God

The poem begins with a famous line: "He is the image of the invisible God" (1:15). This statement is deep, and it is surprisingly difficult to explain. After much consideration, and with some trepidation, I have concluded that Paul is claiming that the Son of God is the divine reflection of God and the revelation of the invisible God to us.

First, "he is" refers to the beloved Son of God mentioned in Colossians 1:13. The NIV brings this out well: "The Son is the image of the invisible God." There has been a tendency in recent scholarship to interpret Colossians 1:15–20 apart from its context because of the theory that Paul is quoting a preexisting hymn. But Fee rightly reminds us that in context, this is a statement about the Son of God.[8]

Second, "he is the image of . . . God" means that the Son is the divine reflection of God. Some interpreters think that Paul is referring to the humanity of Christ because he is alluding to the creation account in which humanity was made in the image of God (Gen. 1:26–28).[9] In this view, the incarnation of the Son has made the invisible God visible. It does seem likely that Paul alludes to the creation account, since an allusion to this account is so clear in the one other use of "image" in

---

6   Most commentaries will display the parallels. See, e.g., G. K. Beale, *Colossians and Philemon*, BECNT (Grand Rapids, MI: Baker Academic, 2019), 100–101.

7   Martin Hengel, *Studies in Early Christology* (New York: T&T Clark International, 1995), xv. "The language of poetry which was inspired by the Spirit breaks the fetters of theological prose and opens the way for new and ever more adventurous statements." Hengel, *Christology*, 285.

8   Gordon D. Fee, *Pauline Christology: An Exegetical-Theological Study* (Peabody, MA: Hendrickson, 2007), 295 and 295n16.

9   For example, N. T. Wright, *The Climax of the Covenant: Christ and the Law in Pauline Theology* (Minneapolis: Fortress Press, 1991), 116.

Colossians (Col. 3:10). It does not follow, however, that the image of God refers to the humanity of the Son.

Instead, Paul roots his claim that the Son is the image of God in the role the Son played in the creation of all things: "For by him all things were created, in heaven and on earth, visible and invisible, whether thrones or dominions or rulers or authorities—all things were created through him and for him" (1:16). The phrases "by him" and "through him" describe the Son as the agent by whom God created all things (cf. 1 Cor. 8:6). And the phrase "for him" describes the Son as the final cause or goal of all creation, language that Paul elsewhere uses of God himself (cf. Rom. 11:36). Thus, as the agent and goal of all creation, the Son of God is the divine reflection of God himself. He is both identified with God as Creator and yet distinguished from God as his reflection.[10]

Third, "he is the image of the *invisible* God" in that the Son reveals God to us. God is "invisible" both in the sense that we cannot see him with our eyes and in the sense that we cannot know him apart from revelation.[11] But the Son of God, as the image of God, has made him known to us, especially in the incarnation.[12] The truth here is complex: the image of God is technically invisible, because it is a reflection of the God who is invisible; and the Son of God is the image of God eternally,

---

10 "By the designation Image of God he is on the one hand distinguished from God, and on the other identified with God as Bearer of the divine glory." Herman Ridderbos, *Paul: An Outline of His Theology*, trans. John Richard de Witt (Grand Rapids, MI: Eerdmans, 1975), 70.

11 Owen comments on the word "invisible" that Paul "intends not only the absolute invisibility of his essence, but his being unknown unto us in himself." John Owen, *The Glory of Christ*, vol. 1, *The Works of John Owen*, ed. William H. Goold (Carlisle, PA: Banner of Truth, 1977), 70.

12 Here I disagree slightly with Tipton and Beale's interpretation of Col. 1:15. They rightly see Paul referring to the Son in his preexistent state but wrongly exclude a reference to the incarnate state as well. See Lane G. Tipton, "Christology in Colossians 1:15–20 and Hebrews 1:1–4: An Exercise in Biblico-Systematic Theology," in *Resurrection and Eschatology: Theology in Service of the Church; Essays in Honor of Richard B. Gaffin Jr.*, ed. Lane G. Tipton and Jeffrey C. Waddington (Phillipsburg, NJ: P&R, 2008), 186–88; Beale, *Colossians and Philemon*, 81–86. This view takes Col. 1:15 out of its context, in which the antecedent of "he" is the incarnate Son (Col. 1:13); and it must distance Col. 1:15 from the parallel text in 2 Cor. 4:4, which clearly refers to the incarnate Christ.

before the incarnation and even before creation (Col. 1:16). But in the incarnation he continues to be the image of God and is the one who reveals God to us.[13] When Paul, for example, saw Jesus in the flesh on the road to Damascus, he saw the Lord (1 Cor. 9:1). And the incarnate Son reveals God not only to our eyes but also to our minds and hearts, as Paul says in a parallel passage: "The god of this world has blinded the minds of the unbelievers, to keep them from seeing the light of the gospel of the glory of Christ, who is the image of God. . . . God, who said, 'Let light shine out of darkness,' has shone in our hearts to give the light of the knowledge of the glory of God in the face of Jesus Christ" (2 Cor. 4:4, 6). When we come to believe in Christ, the image of God, we come to know the invisible God.

Finally, let us briefly consider the biblical-theological relationship of humanity, created in the image of God, and Christ as the image of God. In order to understand this relationship, we must explain both Christ's image-bearing in light of the creation account and the creation account in light of what has now been revealed in Christ. Humanity was made in the image of God in order to rule the world for God (Gen. 1:26–27). But now that the mystery has been revealed in Christ, we can see that human image-bearing was pointing toward a more fundamental and transcendent truth about God that was previously hidden to us. With the coming of Christ we see the "image of God" more clearly in all its transcendent and divine glory. The God who created everything has an image or reflection, a beloved Son, by whom and for whom he created everything. And he is the one whom God always intended to rule over everything in his kingdom (cf. Col. 1:13).

The Firstborn

The rule of the Son is seen more clearly in Paul's next phrase, "the firstborn of all creation" (Col. 1:15). If "the image" shows us his relation to God, "the firstborn" shows us his relation to creation. The phrase is

---

13 Owen helpfully clarifies: "In his incarnation, the Son was made *the representative image* of God unto us—as he was, in his person, *the essential image* of the Father, by eternal generation." Owen, *Works*, 72; emphasis added.

probably better translated "firstborn over all creation" (CSB), for Paul does not say he was the first one to be created but rather that he was the one by whom and for whom all things were created (1:16).[14] So "firstborn" does not speak of his beginning but rather of his preexistence to and thus authority over all creation.

The authority of the Son is comprehensive of all creation. He is firstborn of "*all* creation" (1:15). Paul says twice in Colossians 1:16 that the Son created "*all things*," and then he specifies the comprehensive extent of the "all": "in heaven and on earth, visible and invisible, whether thrones or dominions or rulers or authorities."[15] Finally, he says in Colossians 1:17 that "he is before *all things*," probably referring to temporal priority of the Son and thus his authority over all creation.

Moreover, the authority of the Son has a continuing role in all creation: "In him all things hold together" (1:17). This statement uses one of two perfect-tense verbs in the poem, a tense that communicates a continuing state. The other use is the final statement in Colossians 1:16: "All things *have been created* through him and for him" (NIV). Beasley-Murray comments that "the creation has a permanent and indissoluble relationship to Christ, a relationship which ever seeks to find fulfilment in him."[16] The Son not only has an authoritative role in the beginning and end of creation but in everything in between.

Several scholars have observed that "in him all things hold together" (1:17) is at the center of the two halves of the poem.[17] Perhaps this statement speaks of the Son's role in both creation (1:15–17) and

---

14 Note that the early heresy Arianism appealed to this statement "firstborn of all creation" to prove that the Son was the first one to be created. J. B. Lightfoot, *St. Paul's Epistles to the Colossians and to Philemon* (Lynn, MA: Hendrickson, 1982), 148.

15 This last phrase likely spells out the "invisible" creation in terms of demonic powers, since this was of special concern to the Colossians (cf. "rulers" and "authorities" in Col. 2:15 and Eph. 6:12).

16 Paul Beasley-Murray, "Colossians 1:15–20": An Early Christian Hymn Celebrating the Lordship of Christ," in *Pauline Studies: Essays Presented to Professor F. F. Bruce on His 70th Birthday*, ed. Donald A. Hagner and Murray J. Harris (Grand Rapids, MI: Eerdmans, 1980), 173.

17 For example, Beasley-Murray, "Colossians 1:15–20," 170; Beale, *Colossians and Philemon*, 101–2.

reconciliation (1:18–20). As Creator he is the one who "holds all things together," which ultimately means he will reconcile the parts of creation that have been torn apart in the rebellion. It is interesting that the "first-born" language appears in both halves of the poem. Many suggest that this language comes from the messianic prophecy of Psalm 89: "And I will make him the firstborn, the highest of the kings of the earth" (Ps. 89:27). We see again that "firstborn" refers to his authoritative rule. Paul says the Son began this messianic rule at the resurrection: "He is the beginning, the firstborn from the dead" (Col. 1:18; cf. Rev. 1:5). But he also uses this messianic language of "firstborn" to illuminate the Son's role in creation (Col. 1:15). In this way, the revelation of Christ sheds light on the beginning of history. His resurrection gives us insight into his authoritative role in creation. Now that he has come, we have come to know more clearly who the Creator God is.

The Fullness of God

The Son of God is the key to understanding not only the beginning of history (creation) but also its end (reconciliation). He explains both where we came from and where we are going. Can he really hold all things together (1:17)? Or will it all come flying apart in the end? Closer to home, is our faith in Christ enough to prevent our lives from falling apart? Or do we need to look elsewhere for help? Paul labors to convince the Colossians that they do not need anything else but the Son, because "in him all the fullness of God was pleased to dwell" (1:19).

Colossians 1:19 probably alludes to the Greek translation of Psalm 68:16, where David speaks of the Temple Mount as "the mount that God *desired* for his abode, yes, where the LORD will *dwell* forever."[18] Perhaps Paul's language has also been influenced by the many texts in

---

18 Both Col. 1:19 and Ps. 68:16 speak of the place where God was pleased (*eudokeō*) to dwell (*katoikeō*); and Paul quotes Ps. 68:18 in Eph. 4:8, a letter likely written and sent at the same time as Colossians. For an in-depth discussion of the allusion, see G. K. Beale, "Colossians," in *Commentary on the New Testament Use of the Old Testament*, ed. G. K. Beale and D. A. Carson (Grand Rapids, MI: Baker Academic, 2007), 855–57.

the Old Testament that speak of the glory of God "filling" the temple.[19] The temple was the place where God manifested or revealed his presence in the Old Testament, even though his presence is everywhere (cf. 1 Kings 8:27). Just as God was pleased to dwell in the temple in the Old Testament, so in the incarnation he was pleased to dwell in the human body of his Son so that "in him the whole fullness of deity dwells bodily" (Col. 2:9).

There is, however, a difference in the way God dwelt in the temple and the way that he dwells in the incarnate Son. Paul's point is not simply that God revealed his presence in Jesus. It is not even that God fills all of Christ as he filled the whole temple. Rather, his point is that *all of God* has now come to dwell in Jesus. The adjective "all/the whole" (*pas*) in Colossians 1:19 and 2:9 modifies "fullness," which refers to the full deity of God.[20] Thus all of God has come to dwell in Jesus (1:19); moreover, all of God continues to dwell in the body of Jesus (2:9). Paul does not mean that God is now limited spatially to the body of Christ, because in his divinity Christ is "the One who fills all things in every way" (Eph. 1:23 CSB). Instead, he means that the incarnate Son is and remains fully divine.[21]

And his full divinity entails our fulfillment as well. In Colossians 2:10 Paul continues to use "fullness" language but changes the meaning somewhat: "and you have been filled in him." The idea is that Christ is completely God, so he completes us as well. In him we have true fulfillment, although the exact nature of this fulfillment is unclear.[22] Perhaps

19 Beale lists Ex. 40:34–35; 1 Kings 8:10–11; Isa. 6:4; and many other texts (*Colossians and Philemon*, 177n24).

20 "Fullness" (*plērōma*) should be taken in the passive sense of a filled container rather than the active sense of something that fills. This fits the context, and it is the way *plērōma* is typically used in Paul's letters. Clinton E. Arnold, *The Colossian Syncretism: The Interface between Christianity and Folk Belief at Colossae* (Grand Rapids, MI: Baker, 1996), 262.

21 Note that Col. 2:9 is a classic text for the doctrine of Christ's two natures. Andrew T. Lincoln and A. J. M. Wedderburn, *The Theology of the Later Pauline Letters* (New York: Cambridge University Press, 1993), 64.

22 Blackwell observes that the majority of interpreters see Paul speaking about salvation in general or the fullness of blessing in Christ (Ben C. Blackwell, "You Are Filled in Him: Theosis and Colossians 2–3," *JTS* 8.1 [2004]: 111). His own view is that "being filled in

Paul means that we have been filled with the Spirit of Christ so that we are also the temple of God (cf. Eph. 2:22).[23] This would mean not that we are God but rather that in Christ we are continually in the presence of God. In any case, it is clear that the full deity of Christ is not merely an abstract fact but a life-giving truth for the believer.

It is also a truth that must be lived out. Paul toils in ministry "to make the word of God *fully known*" (Col. 1:25) so that believers will "reach all the riches of *full assurance* of understanding and the knowledge of God's mystery, which is Christ" (2:2). And he prays that the Colossians "may be *filled* with the knowledge of his will" (1:9). As does Epaphras: "Epaphras . . . greets you, always struggling on your behalf in his prayers, that you may stand mature and *fully assured* in all the will of God" (4:12). In these prayers, knowing God's will refers to knowing more deeply his revelation in the fully divine Christ and living in accordance with his lordship. So we see here an example of the indicative-imperative structure of Paul's ethics: believers have been filled in Christ (indicative), so it follows that we must be filled with Christ (imperative).

The Firstborn from the Dead

The incarnation of the Son of God is the basis upon which he has made a new beginning: "He is the beginning, the firstborn from the dead, that in everything he might be preeminent" (1:18). As I observed above, "firstborn" refers to his authoritative rule, alluding to the authority of the Messiah in Psalm 89:27. As Creator he already had authority over all creation by right (Col. 1:15). But in his incarnation and bloody death he has reconciled all things in rebellion to him and won his authority back in fact (1:19–20).[24] On this basis, he has made a new beginning as the

---

Christ entails the embodiment of Christ's death and life, as chaps. 2–3 detail." Blackwell, "Colossians 2–3," 112.

23 So Beale, *Colossians and Philemon*, 178–80.

24 I am indebted to Wright here: "That which he was by right he became in fact" (N. T. Wright, *Colossians and Philemon: An Introduction and Commentary*, TNTC [Downers Grove, IL: InterVarsity Press, 1986], 79). Note also that technically, God has done all this

first of the dead to rise; and he has gained an even greater prominence, a preeminence in everything (1:18).

In this second half of the poem, Paul again emphasizes the Son's comprehensive authority in the work of reconciliation. He is preeminent "in *everything*" (1:18). And he has reconciled "*all* things, whether on earth or in heaven" (1:20). This truth can be difficult to swallow in a world where conflict abounds. Has God really reconciled *all things* through his Son? Here we must remember the hidden nature of his kingdom in the present age: the risen Christ is already reigning above, but his preeminent authority is not yet openly revealed below (3:1–4).

One day, however, it will be fully revealed. For the Son is not only the agent of reconciliation; he is also the goal of reconciliation. Just as all things were created "through him and for him" (1:16), so all things have been reconciled "through him" and "for him" (1:20).[25] It is especially in this language about the Son as the goal of all things that we see his ultimate preeminence. For this is a role that can only be rightly claimed by God himself (cf. Rom. 11:36).

The Head of the Church

Finally, as the firstborn from the dead, "he is the head of the body, the church" (Col. 1:18). In his earlier letters, Paul uses the metaphor of the "body" of Christ to show how the church is both unified and diverse (Rom. 12:4–5; 1 Cor. 12:12–27). In Colossians he continues to use this metaphor to appeal for unity in the church (Col. 3:15); but he also extends the metaphor in saying that Christ is the "head" of the body.[26] In context of the poem, "head" refers to his authoritative role over the church. His temporal priority as the first to be raised results in his preeminent authority in everything. We might compare this with a

---

"through" his Son; but Fee rightly observes that Paul's indirect way of referring to God "*keeps the emphasis on the Son.*" *Pauline Christology*, 311; emphasis original.

25 In Col. 1:20, the phrase *eis auton,* translated by the ESV and most versions as "to himself" (that is, to God), is better translated "for him" (that is, for the Son) in parallel with the first half of the poem (Col. 1:16). So Gordon D. Fee, *Pauline Christology: An Exegetical-Theological Study* (Peabody, MA: Hendrickson, 2007), 311.

26 Cf. 1 Cor. 12:21, where the "head" is one of the members of the body.

founder of a company, who is the head of the company because he or she was the first to start it.

But Paul also uses "head" to refer to Christ as the source of the church's continual growth: "the Head, from whom the whole body, nourished and knit together through its joints and ligaments, grows with a growth that is from God" (2:19). He is the one who bears fruit in our lives (1:6–10) and brings fullness to our lives (cf. 2:10). He is the one who will present us "holy and blameless and above reproach" (1:22). He is the one who is our new life (3:4). There is an indissoluble relationship between Christ and the church, between the head and the body, between the first to be raised and the rest who will be raised. Thus we can never grow beyond Christ but only from Christ and into Christ.

As head of the church, he is also "the head of all rule and authority" (2:10). Paul refers to the demonic powers that were apparently in the forefront of the minds of the Colossians (cf. 1:16; 2:15). The church and her Lord may seem insignificant in the visible world of people, not to mention the invisible world of angels. But the work of reconciliation God has accomplished through the cross is actually bringing all creation back into unity and alignment. The incarnate and risen Son, then, is the authoritative ruler over all people and angels everywhere. And his body, the church, is the most significant body in the world. These statements may sound so extravagant and questionable in our experience that it can be difficult to believe they are true. But we must remember that the gospel is hidden from the world and revealed particularly to the saints (1:26–27). As Paul says elsewhere, it is "a secret and hidden wisdom of God, which God decreed before the ages for our glory" (1 Cor. 2:7). This leads to the final section in the chapter where we see that Christ is the hidden wisdom of God.

The Wisdom of God

One of the most important theological statements in Colossians, and perhaps in all of Paul's letters, is Colossians 2:3: "All the treasures of wisdom and knowledge are hidden in Him" (CSB). After stating this, Paul explains, "I say this in order that no one may delude you with plausible arguments" (2:4). Here we come to the reason Paul wrote to this little church in the Lycus River Valley. The Colossians were in danger of being deluded by a persuasive false teaching that would lead them to look beyond God's Son for deeper or higher wisdom. Paul warns about this false teaching immediately after stating the main point of the letter (2:6–7): "See to it that no one takes you captive by philosophy and empty deceit, according to human tradition, according to the elemental spirits of the world, and not according to Christ" (2:8). He then addresses this philosophy in more detail in Colossians 2:16–23. For modern readers, so far removed from ancient Colossae, it is difficult to know its exact nature, but one thing is clear: it was "not according to Christ"!

The Philosophy

"Philosophy" literally means the love of wisdom or learning. In the modern academy it refers to the study of metaphysics, things beyond the natural order; but in the ancient world it was used more broadly to refer to the study of all reality (including mathematics, for example). If Paul were writing this letter today perhaps he would say, "See to it that no one takes you captive by learning," or, "See that no one takes you captive by scholarship."

Paul is not warning the Colossians that all philosophy or all learning is bad.[27] Instead, he is warning the Colossians that not all learning is "according to Christ." There are some types of philosophy that are fundamentally empty and deceptive (2:8). As I suggested in the prologue, perhaps the false teachers were using the label "philosophy" to lend authority to their teaching, as someone today might use the word *scientific*. Paul tells the Colossians, don't let them take you captive with their persuasive words! Why not?

---

27 Many commentators, in fact, have observed how Paul's language of causality in Col. 1:16 and his "household code" in Col. 3:18–4:1 probably rely to some extent on Greek philosophy.

Human Tradition

First, Paul says this philosophy is "according to human tradition" (2:8). The specific human traditions taught by the philosophy were food restrictions and holiday requirements. Paul warns, "Let no one pass judgment on you in questions of food and drink, or with regard to a festival or a new moon or a Sabbath" (2:16). And he parodies their food restrictions in Colossians 2:21: "Do not handle, Do not taste, Do not touch." As I discussed in the prologue, the false teachers were likely promoting the food and calendar regulations of the Mosaic law. These regulations, Paul again says, are "according to human precepts and teachings" (2:22).

Paul's warning about human tradition is similar to the prophetic critique of Isaiah:

> And the Lord said:
> "Because this people draw near with their mouth
>   and honor me with their lips,
>   while their hearts are far from me,
> and their fear of me is a commandment taught by men,
> therefore, behold, I will again
>   do wonderful things with this people,
>   with wonder upon wonder;
> and the wisdom of their wise men shall perish,
>   and the discernment of their discerning men shall be hidden."
>   (Isa. 29:13–14)

Here the Lord promises to frustrate and destroy the human wisdom of Israel because they are following merely "a commandment taught by men" and not actually drawing near to the Lord with their hearts. Jesus appealed to Isaiah's words when he observed the hypocrisy of the Pharisees, who claimed obedience to God but actually broke the law of God by their traditions (Mark 7:6–12). Paul observes a similar problem: the philosophy claimed to lead people to follow God, but its human wisdom was actually incompatible with Christ, the wisdom of God.

It may seem strange that Paul would identify the holy law of God as "human tradition." Moses describes the law as the God-given path to "wisdom" and "understanding":

> See, I [Moses] have taught you statutes and rules, as the LORD my God commanded me, that you should do them in the land that you are entering to take possession of it. Keep them and do them, for that will be your wisdom and your understanding in the sight of the peoples, who, when they hear all these statutes, will say, "Surely this great nation is a wise and understanding people." For what great nation is there that has a god so near to it as the LORD our God is to us, whenever we call upon him? And what great nation is there, that has statutes and rules so righteous as all this law that I set before you today? (Deut. 4:5–8)

Similarly, the Jewish wisdom tradition describes the law as the pinnacle of divine wisdom:

> All this [wisdom] is the book of the covenant of the Most High God, the law that Moses commanded us as an inheritance for the congregations of Jacob. It overflows, like the Pishon, with wisdom, and like the Tigris at the time of the first fruits. It runs over, like the Euphrates, with understanding, and like the Jordan at harvest time. (Sir. 24:23–26 NRSV)

How then can the apostle Paul describe the law's food and calendar requirements as "*human* tradition"? Because the false teachers, like teachers in the days of Isaiah and Jesus, were teaching the law in the wrong way, in their own way.

Colossians 2:17 is a key verse for understanding why Christians no longer need to keep the food and calendar laws:[28] "These are a shadow of the things to come, but the substance belongs to Christ." Paul is

---

28 I view Col. 2:17 as the ground of the warning about the philosophy in Col. 2:16.

saying that the food and calendar requirements of the law were always intended to point to the reality of Christ.[29] His argument is similar to that of the author of Hebrews: "Since the law has but a shadow of the good things to come instead of the true form of these realities, it can never, by the same sacrifices that are continually offered every year, make perfect those who draw near" (Heb. 10:1). The sacrifices regulated by the Jewish calendar were pointing to the reality of once-for-all sacrifice of Christ for our sins (Heb. 10:14; cf. Col. 1:14).[30] And the clean-and-unclean food requirements were pointing to the Christ whose blood would cleanse our hearts, which is why Jesus declared all foods to be clean (Mark 7:14–23). So the law is indeed the God-given path to wisdom and understanding, but this is because it is the path to Christ![31]

But the false teachers were teaching the law according to human tradition. Apparently, they were teaching that unless the Colossians kept the food restrictions and holidays, they would not be saved (Col. 2:16). But did not the Lord himself teach us that we no longer need to keep the food restrictions (Mark 7:19)? "If only it were that simple," the false teachers might respond. "Yes, we should believe in and follow Christ. But we must also move beyond his teachings to reach the fullness of salvation. There is more to be accessed and experienced in the knowledge of divine things. And one gains access to these things through 'asceticism'" (Col. 2:18, 23). So apparently, the "human tradi-

---

29 The word translated "substance" in Col. 2:17 is *sōma*, which elsewhere in the letter refers to the "body" of Christ (Col. 1:18, 24; 2:19; 3:15). This leads some interpreters to see a reference to the church in Col. 2:17; e.g., Frank Thielman, *Theology of the New Testament: A Canonical and Synthetic Approach* (Grand Rapids, MI: Zondervan, 2005), 380. But as the counterpart to "shadow" it seems more likely that *sōma* means "substance" or "reality" in Col. 2:17.

30 Some Christians believe we are still required to keep the Sabbath holiday in that Sunday is now the Christian Sabbath. In my view, Paul teaches in Col. 2:16–17 that the Sabbath commandment was a shadow that is now fulfilled in Christ. Of course, he also teaches that Christians can "agree to disagree" about such holidays (Rom. 14:5–6). But we should never pass judgment on another Christian for not keeping the Sabbath.

31 In other words, the wisdom of the law was a type of the wisdom of Christ. Beale, *Commentary*, 860.

tion" of the false teachers was their insistence on the food and calendar laws as ascetic ways of humbling the physical body for angelic, visionary experiences (2:18).

The Elemental Spirits

As I discussed in the prologue, some interpreters think that the visions mentioned in Colossians 2:18 were Jewish mystical experiences in which one would enter heaven and join in the angelic worship of God. Others see the visions as pagan experiences in which one would actually worship angels or call upon angelic beings for help in some way. In my view, Paul's reference to "self-made worship" in Colossians 2:23 (my translation) makes it more likely that Colossians 2:18 refers to the human worship of angels in these visions.[32] For many in the ancient world, spiritual forces were thought to hold power and sway over the affairs of life. Perhaps the false teachers were promoting a truly full life through the veneration of these spiritual powers.

But Paul perceives that, ironically, this philosophy that promised salvation from spiritual powers was actually rooted in demonic powers. While at the human level it was "according to tradition," at the spiritual level it was "according to the elemental spirits of the world" (2:8). This difficult phrase is literally "according to the elements of the world" in Greek. Ancient philosophy saw the world as made up of basic elements like earth, water, fire, and air. And these elements were often worshiped by pagans and even personified as spiritual beings. So the "elemental spirits of the world" probably refers to the "rulers and authorities" or demonic powers mentioned in Colossians 1:16; 2:10; and 2:15.[33]

The philosophy, then, was not actually deeper and higher wisdom but human and demonic wisdom. The false teachers claimed that they were leading people into transcendent spiritual realities. But Paul says that anyone who promotes this view is actually "puffed up without cause by a human way of thinking" (2:18 NRSV). The false teachers were "not

---

32 So Beale, *Colossians and Philemon*, 226.
33 Arnold, *Colossian Syncretism*, 193. See his helpful discussion of the issue, which has shaped my view in this paragraph (Arnold, *Colossian Syncretism*, 158–94).

holding fast to the Head" (2:19), the only one from whom true spiritual growth comes. Thus the philosophy did not lead people toward God but away from him, for it was "not according to Christ" (2:8).

All the Hidden Treasures

In contrast, God's Son leads believers into a true knowledge of God, because he is the wisdom of God. The theme of wisdom and knowledge runs throughout Paul's letter to the Colossians. He calls the gospel "the word of the *truth*" and "the grace of God *in truth*" (1:5, 6). He prays that the Colossians will be "filled with the *knowledge* of his will in all spiritual *wisdom* and *understanding*" (1:9). And many have argued that the poem about Christ in Colossians 1:15–20 has been shaped by the Jewish wisdom tradition. For example, in the apocryphal book Wisdom of Solomon, wisdom is personified as "the fashioner of all things" (Wis. 7:22 NRSV),[34] and as "an image of [God's] goodness" (Wis. 7:26 NRSV).[35] But Paul's clearest teaching about Christ as wisdom is found in Colossians 2:1–3:

> For I want you to know how great a struggle I have for you and for those at Laodicea and for all who have not seen me face to face, that their hearts may be encouraged, being knit together in love, to reach all the riches of full assurance of *understanding* and the *knowledge* of God's mystery, which is Christ, *in whom are hidden all the treasures of wisdom and knowledge.*

Moo calls Colossians 2:3 "the christological high point of the letter."[36] I will make several observations about this verse.

First, Christ is the one "in whom" God's wisdom and knowledge are truly found.[37] Second, this wisdom is of immense value, described as

---

34 Cf. Prov. 3:19–20; 8:22–31.

35 Some, however, have questioned whether the wisdom tradition has shaped the poem and Paul's Christology (especially Fee, *Pauline Christology*, 290–91, 317–25, 595–619).

36 Douglas J. Moo, *The Letters to the Colossians and to Philemon*, PNTC (Grand Rapids, MI: Eerdmans, 2008), 169.

37 Cf. Rom. 11:33: "Oh, the depth of the riches and wisdom and knowledge of God!"

"the *treasures* of wisdom and knowledge." Perhaps Paul is dependent on the Old Testament wisdom tradition that often alerts learners to the surpassing value of gaining wisdom. For example, "Blessed is the one who finds wisdom, and the one who gets understanding, for the gain from her is better than gain from silver and her profit better than gold. She is more precious than jewels, and nothing you desire can compare with her" (Prov. 3:13–15). Third, the wisdom found in Christ is not only of immense value but is comprehensive. In him are "*all* the treasures of wisdom and knowledge." One need not and indeed cannot go anywhere else to find God's wisdom. Finally, Paul says that all these treasures are "*hidden*" in Christ. This word could simply refer to the common imagery of hiding a treasure for safe-keeping. But since Paul has just spoken of Christ as the mystery of God in Colossians 2:3, it seems more likely that he is speaking about how God has hidden and revealed his wisdom in his Son. He has been revealed to the saints already in the preaching of the apostles (1:26–27). But he has not been fully revealed, as we see in the next chapter. There is always more treasure to be found in Christ, because all of God is found in him.[38]

Conclusion

In this chapter we have seen Paul's teaching about the preeminence of God's Son from the beginning of creation to the final reconciliation of all things. He is the revelation of God, making known to the saints what was previously hidden. He is the image of God, his divine reflection and revelation to us. He is the fullness of God, in whom all of God was pleased to dwell and under whose headship all things have been reconciled. And he is the wisdom of God, in whom God has hidden all his treasures. Thus we must not look for wisdom

---

38 I think, for example, of the mystery of his divine and human natures united in one person. I have been studying this truth for the past few years in preparation to write this book, and I feel as though I have barely scratched the surface. One resource I have found very helpful is Stephen J. Wellum, *God the Son Incarnate: The Doctrine of Christ* (Wheaton, IL: Crossway, 2016).

beyond the Son, for there is nothing to find beyond him. He is our preeminent hope. And if Christ is preeminent in everything, then he is sufficient for everything in our lives. This latter point is implied in this chapter, but it is spelled out more explicitly in the next chapter.

Christ, Our Life Above

Your life is hidden with Christ in God.
COLOSSIANS 3:3

IN THIS CHAPTER WE SPELL OUT the sufficiency of Christ more clearly by examining Paul's teaching about our new life in Christ. He argues that baptized believers need not submit to any philosophy beyond the preeminent Christ, for we have been buried with him, raised with him, and hidden with him in God above. He is our life, and thus he is our sufficient and hidden hope.

Buried with Christ

The death and burial of Christ are primary elements of the apostolic gospel (see 1 Cor. 15:3–4). All four Gospels recount the burial of Jesus Christ in the tomb of Joseph of Arimathea. His burial is significant because it demonstrates that he really died. Paul appeals to this truth to teach the Colossians that believers in Christ have really died as well, for we have been "buried with him in baptism" (Col. 2:12; cf. Rom. 6:4). When someone dies, it sadly cuts them off from their loved ones, but it also happily cuts them off from their enemies. This latter point is the significance Paul draws out of our burial with Christ. Our baptism symbolizes our union with Christ in his death, in which we have been cut off from all our enemies: our sinful flesh, demonic powers, and even the world.

The Flesh

First, in our burial with Christ we have been cut off from our sinful flesh. Paul uses the imagery of circumcision: "In him also you were circumcised with a circumcision made without hands, by putting off the body of the flesh, by the circumcision of Christ" (Col. 2:11). Circumcision is cutting off of the foreskin on the male sexual organ. It was the visible sign of God's covenant with Abraham, marking Israel as the people of God (Gen. 17:1–14). In Colossians Paul clearly does not refer to physical circumcision, because he says this circumcision was "made without hands." Instead, he refers to the circumcision of the heart, an important theme in biblical theology.

Both the Old and New Testaments teach that God's people must follow him with their whole heart. The law and the prophets chide Israel for being externally marked as God's people but internally far from him: "Circumcise therefore the foreskin of your heart, and be no longer stubborn" (Deut. 10:16); "Circumcise yourselves to the LORD; remove the foreskin of your hearts, O men of Judah and inhabitants of Jerusalem" (Jer. 4:4). In fact, the fundamental reason Israel went into exile was their uncircumcised heart (Lev. 26:41; Jer. 9:25–26). After the exile, however, the Lord promised to circumcise the heart of his people: "The LORD your God will circumcise your heart and the heart of your offspring, so that you will love the LORD your God with all your heart and with all your soul, that you may live" (Deut. 30:6).

Paul tells the Colossians that in Christ they have experienced this promised circumcision. He states it emphatically, mentioning circumcision three times in Colossians 2:11. Were the false teachers promoting circumcision along with food and holiday regulations?[1] It is difficult to

---

1   Yes: N. T. Wright, *Colossians and Philemon: An Introduction and Commentary*, TNTC (Downers Grove, IL: InterVarsity Press, 1986), 109. No: Clinton E. Arnold, *The Colossian Syncretism: The Interface between Christianity and Folk Belief at Colossae* (Grand Rapids, MI: Baker, 1996), 109.

be certain. One thing certain is that the philosophy promoted ascetic bodily disciplines (2:16–18, 20–22). Paul comments, "These have indeed an appearance of wisdom in promoting self-made religion and asceticism and severity to the body, but they are of no value in stopping the indulgence of the flesh" (2:23). So perhaps he emphasizes spiritual circumcision to counter the philosophy's attempt to subdue the sinful flesh through ascetic practices.[2] The only thing that can actually subdue our sinful flesh is the "circumcision made without hands" (2:11).

This circumcision was accomplished at the cross, "by putting off the body of the flesh, by the circumcision of Christ" (2:11). Paul's language is reminiscent of his earlier statement about our reconciliation "in his [Christ's] body of flesh by his death" (1:22). So it seems most likely that he has the same referent in mind: on the cross, Christ himself was circumcised when his fleshly human body was cut off in death.[3] And when he was circumcised, we were circumcised too, because we have been "buried with him in baptism" (2:12). Our sinful flesh was cut off along with his body of flesh. This does not mean that baptized believers are sinless, for Paul goes on to urge believers to put to death our sin (3:5). But it does mean that our sinful flesh no longer has power over us so that we can now obey God from the heart.

Demonic Powers

Second, in our burial with Christ we have been cut off from demonic powers. Paul explains the relationship of demonic powers with the cross in Colossians 2:13–15. This passage is similar to Colossians 1:12–14, which we examined in chapter 1.[4] There, Paul says we have been delivered from the authority of darkness through the forgiveness of our

---

2 Douglas J. Moo, *The Letters to the Colossians and to Philemon*, PNTC (Grand Rapids, MI: Eerdmans, 2008), 197.

3 For this interpretation, which takes "circumcision of Christ" as an objective genitive, see G. K. Beale, *Colossians and Philemon*, BECNT (Grand Rapids, MI: Baker Academic, 2019), 187–91. Alternately, Moo sees a reference to *our* body of flesh and takes "circumcision of Christ" as a possessive genitive (*Colossians and Philemon*, 198–200). This is a difficult verse to interpret.

4 See p. 32.

sins. Here, he says that demonic powers have been disarmed through the forgiveness of our trespasses.[5]

God, in Christ, has "forgiven us all our trespasses, by canceling the record of debt that stood against us with its legal demands" (2:13–14). The words "trespasses" and "legal demands" show that Paul is focusing on violations of the Mosaic law. It is striking that Paul sees the Jewish law making demands on Gentiles, for he has just identified the Colossians as uncircumcised in flesh (2:13). There is a universality to the moral requirements of the law (cf. Rom. 1:32). And our violations of it are recorded as a "record of debt." Paul's point is that God sees and records everything, and his law points out our specific failings, leading to our "record." But in the cross, God has canceled this record: "This he set aside, nailing it to the cross" (Col. 2:14).

As a result, "he disarmed the rulers and authorities and put them to open shame, by triumphing over them in him" (2:15). The word "disarmed" (*apekduomai*) is related to the word translated "putting off" (*akekdusis*) in Colossians 2:11. Although the metaphor has shifted from putting off of clothing to disarming of weapons, the point of both is that the death of Christ has stripped the power of our enemies, whether the flesh or demonic powers.[6] In this verse we see the deep irony of the cross. It would seem that Christ was divested of all power in the cross: disarmed, put to open shame, and triumphed over. But Paul says that the opposite actually happened. In the crucifixion of Christ, God has triumphed over demonic powers. Paul seems to mean that the main power of demons is their ability to tempt us to sin and accuse us of sin. But because God has forgiven "*all* our trespasses" (2:13), demons no longer have *any* power over us. The Colossians, then, need no longer fear these spiritual powers.

The World

Finally, Paul teaches that in our burial with Christ we have been cut off from the world itself. He tells the Colossians that with Christ they "died

---

5   Note how Col. 1:12–14 and 2:13–15 show that the penal substitution and *Christus Victor* theories of the atonement are interwoven in that the former is the basis of the latter.

6   Moo, *Colossians and Philemon*, 214.

to the elemental spirits of the world" and thus they are no longer "alive in the world" (2:20). The spiritual powers associated with the elements of this world are part of the "present evil age" (Gal. 1:4) that is doomed to perish. In this sense they are like the food that the philosophy was so concerned with, which was also doomed to perish (cf. Col. 2:22). But all believers can say with Paul that "the world has been crucified to me, and I to the world" (Gal. 6:14). In Christ, we have been cut off from the old creation and raised to new life in the new creation.

Raised with Christ

The resurrection of Christ is the other primary element of the apostolic gospel (see 1 Cor. 15:4). As the first of the dead to be raised, the Son begins a new era and establishes his absolute preeminence: "He is the beginning, the firstborn from the dead, that in everything he might be preeminent" (Col. 1:18). And those who believe in this "powerful working of God" and are baptized have been "raised with him" (2:12). Thus his resurrection also establishes his sufficiency for our lives in that we have been given new life in him.

Our resurrection with Christ is another way of speaking about our conversion. Paul mixes his metaphors in Colossians 2:11–13. He first speaks of the Colossians having died with Christ and having been raised with him. But then he changes the metaphor by speaking of a resurrection from their own state of deadness: "And you, who were dead in your trespasses and the uncircumcision of your flesh, God made alive together with him" (2:13). This verse is similar to his earlier description of their conversion: "And you, who once were alienated and hostile in mind, doing evil deeds, he has now reconciled" (1:21–22). Before coming to Christ the Colossians were physically alive but they were "dead men walking." For they had transgressed the law of God in their evil deeds and were outside of God's covenant with Abraham in their un-circumcised flesh. They had no chance of standing on the day of God's wrath (cf. 3:6). But now God had made them alive together with Christ.

It is interesting how Paul speaks of our conversion as both a death with Christ and a resurrection with Christ. Our circumcision with

Christ refers to the change of heart God has given us in him. And our resurrection with Christ refers to the new inner life God has given us in him. So we should not make an absolute distinction between our death with Christ and our resurrection with Christ. Both refer to the same reality of our new life in Christ.

Finally, it is important to see that this new life is *resurrection* life. Christ was not raised to the old, fleshly existence like Lazarus so that he might die again. The risen Christ is the beginning of the new creation to come (1:18). So our resurrection with him is part of the new creation as well. Believers are no longer alive in this world (2:20); we are alive in the new creation.

The New Man

Paul describes this new-creation conversion as putting on the new man: "You have put off the [old man] with its practices and have put on the new man, which is being renewed in knowledge after the image of its creator" (3:9–10).[7] These verses clearly allude to the creation of humanity "after the image" (*kat' eikona*) of God in Genesis 1:26–27. It seems likely, then, that Paul is appealing to his well-known parallel between Adam and Christ (cf. Rom. 5:12–21; 1 Cor. 15:20–22, 45–49). The point here is that, in union with the crucified and risen Christ, we have taken off our adamic humanity and put on the new life of Christ like one puts on a new set of clothes.[8]

In the last chapter we learned that Christ is the wisdom of God (Col. 2:3) and the image of God (1:15). We now learn that in Christ *we* are being renewed into the wisdom and image of God. For those in union with Christ have put on the new man, "which is being renewed in knowledge after the image of its creator" (3:10). Paul means that as we come to know Christ more, we are increasing in the knowledge of

---

7   In Col. 3:9–10, I have changed the ESV's "old self" and "new self" to the more literal "old man" (*ton palaion anthrōpon*) and "new man" (*ton neon*).

8   Notice the similar clothing metaphor in Col. 2:11, describing how Christ took off his adamic humanity in the cross: "putting off the body of the flesh." And cf. Gal. 3:27: "For as many of you as were baptized into Christ have put on Christ."

God (cf. 1:10) and thus being shaped into the image of our Creator. He does not mean that we are becoming God but rather that we are becoming like God. Our fallen humanity is being newly made into the image of God. Elsewhere Paul says the believers are being conformed to the image of God's Son (Rom. 8:29; 1 Cor. 15:49; 2 Cor. 3:18). But to become like the Son is to become like God, because he is God.[9]

Further, the term "new man" in Colossians does not refer only to individual believers but to the whole body of Christ. As Paul tells the Corinthians, "*We all* . . . are being transformed" into his image (2 Cor. 3:18). In Colossians 3:11 Paul says that in the new man "there is not Greek and Jew, circumcised and uncircumcised, barbarian, Scythian, slave, free; but Christ is all, and in all." That is, the social divisions that characterized the old creation have been relativized in Christ because he is all that matters in the new creation. "Christ is all" refers to his preeminence in everything (cf. 1:15–20). And "Christ is . . . in all" probably refers to the people in whom he dwells (cf. 1:27).[10] The church is made up of people formally from different social groups (like Philemon and Onesimus), but it is being renewed into a new social group reconciled and united in Christ.

A Future Resurrection in Colossians?

Paul's teaching that believers have been raised with Christ is a major example of the "realized eschatology" of Colossians. This means that the end of time has already been realized in the present. But does it mean that there is nothing left for the future? Some argue that Colossians has almost no place for the future because anything yet to come has already happened in the death and resurrection of Christ:

> When in Colossians and Ephesians baptism signifies that Christians have not only been buried with Christ but have also been raised with Christ in the heavenly places . . . the apocalyptic future collapses into

9   Cf. Owen, following Irenaeus: "He was made like unto us, that we might be made like unto him, and unto God through him." John Owen, *The Glory of Christ*, vol. 1, *The Works of John Owen*, ed. William H. Goold (Carlisle, PA: Banner of Truth, 1977), 1:26.

10 So Moo, *Colossians and Philemon*, 273.

the Christ-event. In this context the church becomes identified with Christ, becoming a heavenly entity and threatening to displace the apocalyptic future. Whereas Rom 6:1–11 limits our present identification with Christ to our participation in his death, Colossians and Ephesians extend it to our participation in his resurrection as well.[11]

This difference between Colossians and Paul's earlier letters is one of the major reasons scholars question whether Paul wrote Colossians.

We must be careful, however, not to overstate the difference. It is true that Paul speaks of the future resurrection in Romans 6: "For if we have been united with him in a death like his, we *shall* certainly be united with him in a resurrection like his" (Rom. 6:5); "if we have died with Christ, we believe that we *will* also live with him" (Rom. 6:8). But he also says that baptized believers possess the new life of the resurrection already: "We were buried therefore with him by baptism into death, in order that, just as Christ was raised from the dead by the glory of the Father, we too might walk in *newness of life*" (Rom. 6:4); "you also must consider yourselves dead to sin and *alive* to God in Christ Jesus" (Rom. 6:11); "present yourselves to God as those who have been brought *from death to life*" (Rom. 6:13). And while Colossians highlights our resurrection with Christ already, it also speaks of the future resurrection of believers: "When Christ who is your life appears, then you also will appear with him in glory" (Col. 3:4). The phrase "in glory" refers to our appearance in the divine, eschatological glory of the resurrection body. This glory was already operative among the Colossians, for Paul prays that they would be "strengthened with all power, according to his *glorious* might, for all endurance and patience with joy" (1:11). But he still speaks of the "hope of glory" (1:27), just as he does in Romans (Rom. 5:2; 8:18–25). So Paul clearly teaches a future resurrection in Colossians.[12]

11 J. Christiaan Beker, *Paul the Apostle: The Triumph of God in Life and Thought* (Philadelphia: Fortress, 1980), 163.

12 Paul also speaks several times of the future, eschatological judgment in the letter (Col. 1:22; 3:6, 24–25).

With that said, there is an emphasis in Colossians on the *realized* aspect of our new life in Christ. There is also an emphasis on the *heavenly* location of our new life in Christ. Paul most likely felt the need to highlight the realized and heavenly aspects of our salvation in order to counter the philosophy's claim that the Colossians must look beyond Christ to angelic visions in order to experience full salvation. In response, Paul says that the Colossians have new life in Christ already and that their life is hidden with Christ in God above. We look at this heavenly and hidden nature of our hope in the final section of the chapter.

Hidden with Christ

The main theme of this book is that Christ is our hidden hope. This theme appears most clearly in Colossians 3:1–4, where Paul reflects on our union with the ascended Christ. Wright calls this "the central passage" in the letter.[13] And Moo says these verses "bring to a climax and summarize much of the key theology of chapters 1–2 as a whole."[14] But the passage also makes an important contribution to the theology of Colossians in its own right, for here Paul explains more clearly the "heavenly eschatology" he introduced in the phrase "the hope laid up for you in heaven" (1:5).[15] In Colossians 3:1–4 we learn more clearly that Christ is our heavenly and hidden hope.

Paul builds his heavenly eschatology on his teaching about our union with the crucified and risen Christ. He again says that "you have been raised with Christ" (3:1) and that "you have died" with Christ (3:3). But he pushes further into the implications of this union by considering our union with Christ in his ascension. For the apostles, the resurrection and ascension of Christ were basically the same theological event. This can be seen in Peter's sermon on Pentecost:

---

13 N. T Wright, *The Resurrection of the Son of God* (Minneapolis: Fortress, 2003), 238.

14 Moo, *Colossians and Philemon*, 244.

15 On heavenly eschatology in Col. 1:5, see pp. 34–35. The poem about the Son also hints at Paul's heavenly eschatology: "For by him all things were created, in *heaven* and on earth" (Col. 1:16).

This Jesus God raised up, and of that we all are witnesses. Being therefore exalted at the right hand of God, and having received from the Father the promise of the Holy Spirit, he has poured out this that you yourselves are seeing and hearing. For David did not ascend into the heavens, but he himself says, "The Lord said to my Lord, 'Sit at my right hand, until I make your enemies your footstool'" [Ps. 110:1]. Let all the house of Israel therefore know for certain that God has made him both Lord and Christ, this Jesus whom you crucified. (Acts 2:32–36)

In summary, Peter says that Jesus has risen and ascended to the throne in heaven, in fulfillment of Psalm 110:1. In Colossians 3:1 Paul alludes to Psalm 110:1 and makes a similar point when he says that "Christ is seated at the right hand of God" (3:1).[16] From this he concludes that believers in union with Christ have ascended with him into heaven as well: "You have died, and *your life is hidden with Christ in God*" (3:3). Since this is one of the major theological contributions of Colossians, I will take it phrase by phrase.

First, Paul says that the ascended Christ is "your life." He tells the Colossians they have died but that paradoxically they still live. This is similar to what he says of himself in Galatians 2:20: "I have been crucified with Christ. It is no longer I who live, but Christ who lives in me." The glorious and rich mystery of the gospel is that Christ lives in us (by his Spirit) (Col. 1:27). Yet in Colossians 3:3 Paul does not speak about Christ living in us below, but rather about believers living in Christ above. So it is true not only that we believers have the new life of the resurrection within us but also that our new life is in heaven, for Christ "is your life" (3:4).

---

16 I have removed the ESV's comma between "Christ is" and "seated," because I think it is more likely that "is" (*estin*) and "seated" (*kathēmenos*) is a periphrastic construction communicating one idea; so A. T. Robertson, *A Grammar of the Greek New Testament in the Light of Historical Research*, 4th ed. (New York: George H. Doran, 1923), 881. Note, however, that most translations and commentators agree with the ESV (Moo, *Colossians and Philemon*, 247).

Second, Paul says our life has been "hidden."[17] In the context of Colossians, "hidden" most likely means that our new lives are not yet openly revealed. Just as God has hidden the gospel from the beginning of time (1:26) and has hidden all the treasures of wisdom in Christ (2:3), so he has hidden the lives of baptized believers with Christ above (3:3). Although it is true that we already have resurrection life with Christ, believers await the open revelation of our resurrection glory at the revelation of Christ: "When Christ who is your life appears, then you also will appear with him in glory" (3:4).[18] The believer's hope is "laid up . . . in heaven" (1:5), which means that the believer's hope is not yet revealed.[19] It is a heavenly and thus hidden hope. This is a call to walk by faith and not by sight (cf. the main point of the letter in 2:6).

Third, Paul says that our life is "hidden with Christ in God." The reason our lives are hidden above is our union with the ascended Christ. He is sufficient to bring us to God. The philosophy apparently promoted legalism and mysticism as a means of heavenly ascent. But Paul says that the crucified, risen, and ascended Christ has already brought us to God. In him, we are as close to God as we can possibly be, even though this truth is not yet openly revealed.

Finally, many interpreters see the notion of safety in the phrase "your life is hidden with Christ in God."[20] Comparison is often made with Old Testament texts like Psalm 27:4–5:

---

17 This perfect-tense verb is more literally translated "has been hidden." Lightfoot comments on Col. 3:3 that "the aorist ['you died'] denotes the past act; the perfect ['you have been hidden'] the permanent effects." J. B. Lightfoot, *St. Paul's Epistles to the Colossians and to Philemon* (Lynn, MA: Hendrickson, 1982), 209.

18 Cf. Phil. 3:20–21: "But our citizenship is in heaven, and from it we await a Savior, the Lord Jesus Christ, who will transform our lowly body to be like his glorious body, by the power that enables him even to subject all things to himself."

19 Foster observes, "The major contrast between these two realities [of heaven and the world] seems to be that things in the heavens remain invisible while things in the world (cosmos) are visible." Robert L. Foster, "Reoriented to the Cosmos: Cosmology and Theology in Ephesians through Philemon," in *Cosmology and New Testament Theology*, LNTS 355, ed. Jonathan T. Pennington and Sean M. McDonough (New York: T&T Clark International, 2008), 114.

20 E.g., Arnold, *Colossian Syncretism*, 307.

One thing have I asked of the LORD,
  that will I seek after:
that I may dwell in the house of the LORD
  all the days of my life,
to gaze upon the beauty of the LORD
  and to inquire in his temple.

For he will *hide* me in his shelter
  in the day of trouble;
he will conceal me under the cover of his tent;
  he will lift me high upon a rock.

It is not clear to me that "hide" in Psalm 27:5 is being used in quite the same way as in Colossians 3:3, for the primary meaning in Paul is not being hidden from trouble but being hidden in heaven and waiting to be revealed. Nevertheless, Paul's whole statement surely resonates with David's prayer and implies that our lives are safe with Christ in God.

Contribution to Pauline Theology

Colossians makes a distinct contribution to Paul's theology in its emphasis on the heavenly aspect of the realized eschatology. Paul's realized eschatology is a paradox (already–not yet) but not a contradiction. Nor is it a mysterious antinomy that we cannot fully explain, like God's sovereignty and human responsibility. Rather, the hope of the gospel is "already" in one sense and "not yet" in another sense.

In Paul's letters, we can often explain this already–not yet paradox with an internal-external framework. Believers already have resurrection life internally, but we do not yet have resurrection life externally (Rom. 8:9–11; 2 Cor. 4:16–18).[21] The Spirit of God dwells within us, and we are being transformed into the image of Christ; but we await the day when we will be fully transformed into his resurrection likeness.

---

21 My argument here has been influenced by Richard B. Gaffin Jr., *By Faith, Not by Sight: Paul and the Order of Salvation*, 2nd ed. (Phillipsburg, NJ: P&R, 2013), 61–67.

In Colossians we continue to see this internal-external framework. The mystery is "Christ in you [internal], the hope of glory [external]" (Col. 1:27). But we also see an above-below framework. Believers already have resurrection life above, but it is not yet revealed below. This heavenly eschatology is not entirely unique to Paul's letter to the Colossians, for in Galatians he speaks of the "Jerusalem above" (Gal. 4:26).[22] But the philosophy in Colossae led Paul to draw out the implications of Christ's ascension in a distinct way.[23] Christ is our hidden hope both within and above.

Conclusion

In this chapter we have considered the sufficiency of Christ by examining Paul's teaching about our new life in Christ. Baptized believers have been buried with Christ so that we are cut off from our enemies: the flesh, demonic powers, and even the world. We have been raised with Christ so that we have new life that is being renewed after the image of God. And our lives have been hidden with the ascended Christ in God and will one day be revealed with him in resurrection glory. What more do we need? All we need now is to continue to walk in our sufficient Christ, a "walk" we examine at length in the next chapter.

---

22 Heavenly eschatology is not unique to Paul either. The book of Revelation, for example, envisions the heavenly throne that will one day come to earth. And the Jewish apocalypse of Baruch speaks of the heavenly Jerusalem that will one day be revealed (*2 Bar.* 4:1–7).

23 "The syncretistic teaching simply draws out an emphasis on the heavenly realm which is already inherent in Paul's eschatological perspective." Andrew T. Lincoln, *Paradise Now and Not Yet: Studies in the Role of the Heavenly Dimension in Paul's Thought with Special Reference to His Eschatology*, SNTSMS 43 (New York: Cambridge University Press, 1981), 131.

4

Christ, Our Life Below

Do everything in the name of the Lord Jesus.

COLOSSIANS 3:17

IN THIS CHAPTER WE EXAMINE Paul's ethical instructions in Colossians, which are central to his main appeal to "walk" in Christ (Col. 2:6) and make up a substantial portion of the letter. Paul's theological teaching that "your life is hidden with Christ in God" (3:3) may sound esoteric and impractical. For Paul, however, it is this indicative reality of our new life in Christ that must form the basis of our daily Christian "walk." The hidden hope of Christ should motivate us to seek the things above, put earthly things to death, put on the new man, and do everything in the name of the Lord Jesus.

Seek the Things Above

On the basis of their resurrection with the ascended Christ, Paul appeals to the Colossians to "seek the things that are above" (3:1). Very similar is his accompanying command to "set your minds on things that are above" (3:2). Paul is speaking about the things believers should think about with their minds and aspire to in their actions. Those who have been united with the ascended Christ should be heavenly minded and heavenly oriented. Our feet may be on the ground, but our heads must be in heaven. We should not meditate on and focus on things below but on things above.

What are the heavenly things that believers should think about and seek after? First and foremost is Christ, who is seated in heaven at the right hand of God (3:1). Christ should be constantly on our minds, and his glory should be the motivating factor of all that we do. This accords with God's own purpose of creating all things "for him" (1:16) and reconciling all things "for him" (1:20, my translation). We have been created and redeemed "for him."

But "the things above" is also a broader category that includes every thought and action that is a part of our new life in Christ. Paul draws a contrast between the "things that are above" and the "things that are on earth" (3:2). He then defines "what is earthly in you" as the vices of sexual immorality and anger that characterized our former life (3:5–11). In contrast, "the things above" are the thoughts and actions of the new life spelled out in Colossians 3:12–4:6. Keener rightly concludes that "Colossians speaks of no abstract contemplation detached from present earthly existence. Rather, the focus on heaven is a focus on Christ, not only as he is enthroned above, but as that reality of his lordship impinges on daily life."[1]

In Colossians 3:1–11 we see an example of the indicative-imperative paradox that is characteristic of Paul's ethical instructions. Paul can state the same truth as both an indicative fact of the gospel and an imperative command arising from the gospel. For Paul, believers have new life in Christ (indicative), so they must seek new life in Christ (imperative). Wright comments, "The new life, to be revealed fully on the last day (v. 4), is to let itself be seen in advance, in the present time, in Christian behaviour."[2] Believers must diligently pursue the new life of the resurrection, like Paul: "Not that I have already obtained this [the resurrection] or am already perfect, but I press on to make it my

---

1   Craig S. Keener, *The Mind of the Spirit: Paul's Approach to Transformed Thinking* (Grand Rapids, MI: Baker, 2016), 246.

2   N. T. Wright, *Colossians and Philemon: An Introduction and Commentary*, TNTC (Downers Grove, IL: InterVarsity Press, 1986), 138.

own, because Christ Jesus has made me his own. . . . Let those of us who are mature think this way" (Phil. 3:12, 15).

Put Earthly Things to Death

The first step in this pursuit is a radical one: "Put to death therefore what is earthly in you" (Col. 3:5). Notice that the indicative leads to the imperative: "You have died" (3:3); therefore, "put to death" (3:5).[3] Our sinful flesh cannot be stopped through ascetic practices (2:23) but only through the circumcision of Christ and our death and burial with him (2:11–12; 3:3). This is the indicative. But now we see the imperative: believers must now put to death what is earthly in them in order to live the new life of Christ.

Literally Paul says, "Put to death your members that are on the earth" (3:5, my translation). These "members" are the vices that have characterized our lives, like "sexual immorality" (3:5). In this way Paul teaches us that our sinful desires and actions cannot be divorced from our person but are in a sense "members" of our body. Lohse comments, "Man cannot distance himself from his actions; he is so intimately bound up with them that his actions are a part of himself."[4] Therefore, the call to put to death these vices is really a call to crucify ourselves—that is, our old, adamic humanity, the ways in which "you too once walked, when you were living in them" (3:7). These ways are characteristic of our former life below rather than our new life above. And Paul solemnly warns that "on account of these the wrath of God is coming" (3:6). What are "these"?

There are two vice lists, and the first focuses on our sexual transgression and desires: "sexual immorality, impurity, passion, evil desire, and covetousness, which is idolatry" (3:5). The final vice, covetousness, is added as a natural progression since sexual transgression is often

---

3 Wedderburn observes that Col. 3:3 and 5 state "the paradox of indicative and imperative with a sharpness almost unparalleled in Paul's writings." Andrew T. Lincoln and A. J. M. Wedderburn, *The Theology of the Later Pauline Letters* (New York: Cambridge University Press, 1993), 54.

4 Eduard Lohse, *Colossians and Philemon*, Hermeneia, trans. William R. Poehlmann and Robert J. Karris (Philadelphia: Fortress, 1971), 137.

rooted in the desire for what does not belong to us. "Covetousness" refers, however, to greed for money and possessions, since greed was often associated with idolatry in Jewish and Christian literature (cf. Job 31:24–28; Matt. 6:24).[5] Paul claims that greed *is* idolatry, meaning that like idolatry it "is an attack on God's exclusive rights to human love and devotion, trust and confidence, and service and obedience."[6] Greed and sexual transgression are often trivialized today, but Paul warns that believers must put them to death or risk facing the wrath of God.

Paul's second vice list focuses on our anger that often spills over into our speech: "But now you must put them all away: anger, wrath, malice, slander, and obscene talk from your mouth" (Col. 3:8). Regarding the first three vices, Moo comments that "Paul's purpose is not to single out three specific sins but to use the three words together to connote the attitude of anger and ill will toward others that so often leads to hasty and nasty speech."[7] In our anger we can also easily misrepresent the facts and "slander" our neighbor. And we can feel warranted to speak in a derogatory way that is colored by "obscene" words. This kind of speech foments division in the church, which is (and thus should be) one man in Christ (see 3:11). All these things must now be put to death by believers. Or, using a clothing metaphor, Paul says "you must put them all away" (3:8).[8]

Put on the New Man

In the clothing metaphor we see another example of the indicative-imperative structure of Paul's ethical instructions in Colossians. In the last chapter we learned that Christ has put off his fleshly body in

---

5   See Brian S. Rosner, *Greed as Idolatry: The Origin and Meaning of a Pauline Metaphor* (Grand Rapids, MI: Eerdmans, 2007).

6   This is the conclusion of Rosner's study (*Greed as Idolatry*, 173; original emphasis removed).

7   Douglas J. Moo, *The Letters to the Colossians and to Philemon*, PNTC (Grand Rapids, MI: Eerdmans, 2008), 264.

8   It seems likely to me that Col. 3:8 uses a clothing metaphor, since the same metaphor is used in Col. 3:9–10; but some commentators disagree (e.g., Moo, *Colossians and Philemon*, 262–63).

the cross (2:11) and that, with him, believers have put off the old man, our old adamic humanity, and put on the new man, our new life in Christ (3:9–10).[9] On this basis, Paul gives an imperative against lying: "Do not lie to one another" (3:9). But he also gives imperatives that paradoxically reuse the clothing metaphor. The indicative you "have put on" in Colossians 3:10 leads to the imperative "put on then . . ." in Colossians 3:12–14. The Colossians *have* put on the new man, so now they *must* put on the new man.[10]

How can they do this? By putting on the virtues exemplified by the Lord himself: "compassionate hearts, kindness, humility, meekness, and patience" (3:12). Reading this list we are reminded of the "clothes" worn by Christ throughout the Gospels. As he said, "Take my yoke upon you, and learn from me, for I am gentle and lowly in heart" (Matt. 11:29).[11] Surely we need the resurrection life of heaven to be able to follow him in these remarkable virtues. Putting on these clothes should also lead to a new man corporately: "bearing with one another and, if one has a complaint against another, forgiving each other" (Col. 3:13). Forgiveness is at the heart of the gospel (cf. 1:14), and it must be a hallmark of the new life. The Lord taught us this in his prayer (Matt. 6:12) and his parable of the unforgiving servant (Matt. 18:21–35). In that parable the lord of the servant asks, "Should not you have had mercy on your fellow servant, as I had mercy on you?" (Matt. 18:33). Similarly, Paul teaches that "as the Lord has forgiven you, so you also must forgive" (Col. 3:13).

Paul saves the most important virtue for last: "And above all these put on love, which binds [everyone] together in perfect harmony"

---

9   A minority of commentators argue that the participles "put off" and "put on" in Col. 3:9–10 should be taken as imperatives because of the parallel passage in Eph. 4:20–24 (e.g., Lohse, *Colossians and Philemon*, 141). But it is much more likely that the participles are adverbial participles of cause, giving the indicative reason why we should not lie to one another (so Moo, *Colossians and Philemon*, 265–66n66).

10 Cf. Rom. 13:14: "Put on the Lord Jesus Christ, and make no provision for the flesh, to gratify its desires."

11 For this point, I am indebted to Gordon D. Fee, *Pauline Christology: An Exegetical-Theological Study* (Peabody, MA: Hendrickson, 2007), 328.

(3:14).[12] Love is the bond that unites the church (cf. 1:4). Thus it brings God's plan for the new man to perfection. He has reconciled all things through and for his Son (1:20). This reconciliation was working itself out through Paul's labors as believers were "knit together in love" (2:2). And it continues to work itself out today as believers put on love as the highest and most Christlike of the virtues.

We can engage in the difficult task of love because we are loved by God. Paul reminds the Colossians that they are "God's chosen ones, holy and beloved" (3:12). He likens them to Israel in the Old Testament:

> For you are a people holy to the LORD your God. The LORD your God has chosen you to be a people for his treasured possession, out of all the peoples who are on the face of the earth. It was not because you were more in number than any other people that the LORD set his love on you and chose you, for you were the fewest of all peoples, but it is because the LORD loves you and is keeping the oath that he swore to your fathers, that the LORD has brought you out with a mighty hand and redeemed you from the house of slavery, from the hand of Pharaoh king of Egypt. (Deut. 7:6–8)

These uncircumcised Gentiles in the backwater town of Colossae had become the redeemed and beloved people of God. How was this possible? Because they were in his beloved Son, so now they must put on their new life in him.

Do Everything in His Name

The Christological focus of Paul's ethical instructions becomes even more prominent in Colossians 3:15–17 where he speaks of "the peace

12 I have changed the ESV's "which binds *everything* together" to "which binds *everyone* together" in Col. 3:14. The Greek literally says that love "is the bond of perfection." Some scholars think Paul refers to love as that which perfectly binds together all the virtues (e.g., Moo, *Colossians and Philemon*, 281–82). But it seems more likely that Paul means that love perfectly binds together the church in a context that so stresses the unity of the new man (and cf. Col. 2:2, 19); so David W. Pao, *Colossians and Philemon*, ZECNT (Grand Rapids, MI: Zondervan Academic, 2012), 245.

of Christ," "the word of Christ," and "the name of the Lord Jesus." Paul's ethical teaching is not simply added to his theological teaching in the letter. Rather, it naturally flows out of the truth of the preeminence and sufficiency of Christ. The lordship of Christ touches every area of our lives, and his new life enables us for anything we may encounter in our lives.

First, "the peace of Christ" must unify the body of Christ: "And let the peace of Christ rule in your hearts, to which indeed you were called in one body" (3:15). God has made peace by the blood of his Son (1:20). He has called us to unity in one body, the body of his Son. It is this divine reconciliation in Christ, then, that must control our hearts, not the traditions of men or angels (cf. 2:18).[13]

Second, "the word of Christ" must dwell in us and spill over to others: "Let the word of Christ dwell in you richly, teaching and admonishing one another in all wisdom, singing psalms and hymns and spiritual songs, with thankfulness in your hearts to God" (3:16). The "word of Christ" refers to the message about Christ, "the word of the truth, the gospel" (1:5).[14] Christ is the one "in whom are hidden all the treasures of wisdom and knowledge" (2:3), and his indwelling presence is of immeasurable value (1:27). Thus we must treasure up the gospel of Christ in our hearts so that it spills over into wise instruction and thankful singing. Paul exemplified this command as he sat in prison: he let the word of Christ dwell richly in him, and it spilled over into the wise instruction of this letter.[15] One imagines that it spilled over into thankful singing as well (cf. Acts 16:25).

---

13 Note that there is probably a connection between "disqualify" (*katabrabeuō*) in Col. 2:18 and "rule" (*brabeuō*) in Col. 3:15.

14 "In light of Col. 1:5–6 where 'the word of truth' is identified as 'the gospel that has come to you,' the 'word of Christ' in 3:16 should not be understood as referring to individual sayings of Jesus but to the gospel message as a whole." David W. Pao, *Thanksgiving: An Investigation of a Pauline Theme*, NSBT 13 (Downers Grove, IL: InterVarsity Press, 2002), 114n85.

15 Cf. Col. 1:28, where Paul uses the same verbs translated "teaching" (*didaskō*) and "admonishing" (*noutheteō*) in Col. 3:16 to describe his own calling: "Him we proclaim, warning [*nouthetountes*] everyone and teaching [*didaskontes*] everyone with all wisdom, that we may present everyone mature in Christ."

Third, "the name of the Lord Jesus" must guide everything we say and do: "And whatever you do, in word or deed, do everything in the name of the Lord Jesus, giving thanks to God the Father through him" (Col. 3:17). As servants of Jesus, he is our Lord and we are his representatives. So we should do everything in his name. This imperative is comprehensive, but it is also mundane, referring to our everyday lives. Lohse comments that "it is precisely in the Christian's everyday life, where he toils and sweats, that he is placed under the command to prove his allegiance to the Lord."[16] The burden of this command, however, is light, for it is done in thanksgiving to the Father, who has brought us into the kingdom of his Son.[17]

Christ's Lordship in the Home

It is likely that Paul intended his next set of instructions, in Colossians 3:18–4:1, to be an explanation of what it means to "do everything in the name of the Lord Jesus" (3:17). The lordship of Christ is a prominent theme in this section, as can be seen from the repeated use of "Lord." The passage is a "household code," addressing differing relationships of authority within the home. How can Paul affirm these differences in light of his egalitarian teaching that in the new man "there is not Greek and Jew, circumcised and uncircumcised, barbarian, Scythian, slave, free" (3:11; cf. Gal. 3:28; 1 Cor. 12:13)? Assuming that Paul does not contradict himself, we must understand Paul's egalitarian statement in a relative sense rather than in an absolute sense. Moo comments that "the distinctions of this world, while not obliterated, are relativized."[18] Each believer must continue to live in the differing social conditions

---

16 Lohse, *Colossians and Philemon*, 153.

17 Barclay comments, "Not only does the act of thanksgiving reorientate the believer to the divine reality, it also implies the acceptance of present conditions as those in which Christ can be worshipped and served. Thus to 'do everything in the name of the Lord Jesus, *thanking God through him*' (3:17) is to reaffirm the reality of the Lordship of Christ, in creation and redemption, and thus to reinforce the sense that it is possible and glorious to serve Christ in what is truly his own domain. Thankfulness makes life both purposeful and hopeful." John M. G. Barclay, "Ordinary but Different: Colossians and Hidden Moral Identity," *ABR* 49 (2001): 46–47.

18 Moo, *Colossians and Philemon*, 272.

in which he or she was called (cf. 1 Cor. 7:17–24). But these differences are relativized in that Christ is our common Lord, and we are brothers and sisters in him (cf. Philem. 16).[19]

The instructions for wives, husbands, children, and fathers are straightforward. Wives are called to submit to their husbands, to give deference to their leadership, because it "is fitting in the Lord" (Col. 3:18).[20] Husbands are instructed to love their wives and warned to "not be harsh with them" (3:19). We recall that Christ is "gentle and lowly in heart" (Matt. 11:29; cf. Col. 3:12) and that love is the supreme virtue of our new life in him (Col. 3:14). Children are instructed, "Obey your parents in everything, for this pleases the Lord" (3:20). The verb "obey" is a different word in Greek than "submit," showing that Paul sees nuance in the authority structures of the household. And "in everything" does not include the hopefully rare occasions when parents order children to disobey the Lord, for how could that please him? Finally, fathers are warned to put to death their flesh in parenting: "Do not provoke your children, lest they become discouraged" (3:21).

Over half the household instructions are addressed to slaves and masters (3:22–4:1).[21] These instructions are probably where modern

---

19 Thielman helpfully observes that "Paul does not legitimate his household order by finding something intrinsically inferior about its subordinate members. He refuses even to say that children are immature. The household code in Paul's letter, therefore, is integrated into the theme of social reconciliation that pervades the entire section from 3:5 to 4:1 and that is, in turn, a reflection of the reconciliation God has effected with the universe through Christ's death. In the Christian household, as in the church, a common equality undergirds the ordering of relationships because 'Christ is all, and is in all' (3:11)." Frank Thielman, *Theology of the New Testament: A Canonical and Synthetic Approach* (Grand Rapids, MI: Zondervan, 2005), 384.

20 This instruction is controversial today and much debated in the commentaries, where one can go for further discussion. It is worth observing that Paul is not instructing every woman in the church to submit to every man but only wives to submit to their husbands.

21 The ESV translates *douloi* with "bondservants" in Col. 3:22. But Harris argues that *doulos* should always be translated "slave" in the household codes because the mention of masters shows that slavery is in view (Murray J. Harris, *Slave of Christ: A New Testament Metaphor for Total Devotion to Christ*, NSBT 8 [Downers Grove, IL: InterVarsity Press, 1999], 188). See his whole discussion of the translation issue on pp. 183–91. Note also his definition of a slave: "someone whose person and service belong wholly to another." *Slave of Christ*, 25.

readers feel most the historical "otherness" of the letter. I address the question of slavery below and in the next chapter. For now I simply attempt to describe Paul's instructions. The bulk of his instructions are given to slaves, likely as a counterweight to Philemon.[22] The letter to Philemon was not simply written to an individual but to the whole church, and it would likely have been read at the same time as Colossians.[23] Paul's instructions in that letter appeal to Philemon to welcome Onesimus and forgive his wrongdoing, using the verb *adikeō*, "to do wrong" (Philem. 18). In Colossians Paul uses the same verb to instruct slaves to obey their masters, warning that at the final judgment "the wrongdoer [*adikōn*] will be paid back for the wrong he has done [*ēdikēsen*], and there is no partiality" (3:25).[24] Thus, whereas in Philemon Paul urges a master to forgive his slave, in Colossians he warns slaves that such forgiveness is not a license for wrongdoing.

The lordship of Christ shines out most clearly in Paul's instructions to slaves and masters. In these verses, Paul uses the word *kurios* seven times, translated in the ESV with both "master" and "lord." Christ's lordship relativizes the authority of earthly masters in two ways. First, he is the ultimate master of Christian slaves. Thus they should obey their earthly masters in everything, not "as people-pleasers" but rather because they fear "*the* Lord" (3:22).[25] They should work hard "not for men" but "for the Lord" (3:23). And they should "serve the Lord

---

22 So J. B. Lightfoot, *St. Paul's Epistles to the Colossians and to Philemon* (Lynn, MA: Hendrickson, 1982), 229. *Pace* Lincoln, who interestingly suggests that the instructions to slaves receive the most attention because they are paradigmatic of how all Christians should serve Christ. Andrew T. Lincoln, "The Household Code and the Wisdom Mode of Colossians," *JSNT* 74 (1999): 105–6.

23 The letter is addressed to the church that met in Philemon's house (Philem. 2), probably the whole church at Colossae or perhaps one of its house churches. And in its closing grace wish (Philem. 25), the words "your spirit" are plural in Greek.

24 Some commentators take Col. 3:25 as a warning to masters (or to both slaves and masters), but "Paul does not explicitly turn to address 'masters' until the next verse" (Moo, *Colossians and Philemon*, 314).

25 As I qualified the instruction to children, obeying "in everything" (Col. 3:22) surely does not include times when a master asks a slave to disobey his or her ultimate Lord. For example, Joseph disobeyed Potiphar's wife (Gen. 39). For this example, I am indebted

Christ"[26] with an eye toward his final coming, when he will reward the saints with their final inheritance (3:24; cf. 1:12) and pay back the wrongdoers without partiality (3:25). In saying all this, Paul ennobles the mundane and difficult work of slaves by reminding them of their heavenly master who will one day be revealed (cf. 3:1–4). Barclay observes that "the Christian slave can find even in such difficult circumstances a rationale and goal for life. Thus the code indicates how even the most unpromising circumstances in life can become an arena in which the mystery of Christ is recognized and served."[27] Second, the lordship of Christ relativizes the authority of earthly masters because they are also slaves of the Lord in heaven (4:1; cf. 1 Cor. 7:22). Thus they should treat their slaves "justly and fairly," for one day his hidden, heavenly lordship will be revealed.

Slavery in Biblical Theology

Modern Christians often wonder why Paul did not simply command Christian masters to free their slaves and let that be that. In 1 Corinthians 7:21–23 Paul counsels Christian slaves to pursue freedom if they can, so perhaps one issue is that these slaves and masters didn't have the option to pursue freedom immediately. Some slaves in the Colossian church were probably enslaved to unbelievers. Others might not have been able to support themselves if they were released from their master's household. The first-century philosopher Epictetus, who had been a slave himself, observes that every slave prays to be freed immediately but that his "freedom" might actually lead to a worse condition,

---

to Esau McCaulley, *Reading While Black: African American Biblical Interpretation as an Exercise in Hope* (Downers Grove, IL: IVP Academic, 2020), 161.

26 Most English translations render *doulete* in Col. 3:24 as an indicative verb: "you are serving the Lord Christ." But most commentaries view it as an imperative verb: "serve the Lord Christ" (Moo, *Colossians and Philemon*, 313).

27 John M. G. Barclay, *Colossians and Philemon*, T&T Clark Study Guides (New York: T&T Clark International, 1997), 91. I should note that Barclay is taking Col. 3:25 as a warning to both slaves and masters, and noting how slaves may experience wrongdoing from masters. Although I disagree with his interpretation of this verse, it is certainly correct that slaves were often treated wrongly and unfairly.

like earning a living by prostitution.[28] Others may have simply been waiting for the future, since it was common in the ancient world to free slaves eventually. In this way, ancient slavery was different from modern slavery in America. Still, does that make it right? I cannot fully answer this question, of course, but here I will attempt to state briefly my understanding of slavery in biblical theology.

Slavery is never treated as part of the "very good" creation of God (cf. Gen. 1:31). In fact, it is treated as the opposite—a curse from which God must redeem his people. The first reference to slavery in the Bible is the curse of Canaan (Gen. 9:25), as some of the church fathers observed.[29] It should be emphatically stated, however, that this verse is not teaching about modern racial distinctions, as some have attempted to interpret it. My point is simply that slavery is associated not with the blessing of creation but with the curse of the fall.

The exodus, Israel's redemption from slavery in Egypt, looms large in biblical theology (Ex. 1–15). It is the greatest act of redemption in the Old Testament and becomes the most important type of redemption in the Bible (cf. Col. 1:12–14). The Mosaic law repeatedly reminds Israel of this event (e.g., Ex. 20:2), and it forbids the perpetual slavery of fellow Israelites because the Lord had redeemed them for himself (Lev. 25:38, 55; Deut. 15:15). It does, however, tolerate and regulate slavery, and even the perpetual slavery of foreigners (e.g., Lev. 25:45–46).[30] In my view, the law tolerates and regulates slavery in the same way that it tolerates and regulates divorce. Jesus taught us that Moses wrote about divorce to regulate Israel's hardness of heart, even though divorce cuts against the creation design of monogamous marriage between a man and a woman (Mark 10:1–12; cf. Deut. 24:1–4). Jesus and the apostles also tolerated and regulated divorce in the extreme cases of adultery and abandonment (Matt. 5:32; 19:9; 1 Cor. 7:15). Similarly, slavery is tolerated and regulated in the Old and New Testaments, even though

---

28 Epictetus, *Diatr.* 4.33–40.
29 Mitchell notes that this was a common explanation among the church fathers. Margaret M. Mitchell, "John Chrysostom on Philemon: A Second Look." *HTR* 88:1 (1995): 135–48.
30 For the laws about slaves, see Ex. 21; Lev. 25; and Deut. 15.

it cuts against God's creation design and his great act of redemption in Christ.[31]

Finally, God has redeemed the institution of slavery by using it as a metaphor for our new relationship with Christ. Paul identifies the man who carried these two letters, Tychicus, as "a beloved brother and faithful minister and fellow slave in the Lord" (Col. 4:7, my translation). He identifies Epaphras as "our beloved fellow slave" (1:7, my translation) and "a slave of Christ Jesus" (4:12, my translation). And he says that both slaves and masters have a master in heaven (4:1), implying that we are all slaves of Christ. Harris observes, "However much we moderns, living on the other side of the abolition of slavery, may be scandalized by the New Testament use of the image of slavery to depict one aspect of our ideal relationship to the Deity, we cannot eradicate such imagery from the New Testament without compromising its message."[32] We can contrast this message with another approach taken to slavery in the ancient world. Some philosophers argued that slaves can be free in the soul even while enslaved in the body. But Paul offers a better hope, the hope of the gospel, that Christian slaves ultimately belong body and soul to the Lord Christ.[33]

This is a hope that must be communicated to everyone. Paul closes his ethical instructions in Colossians 3:1–4:6 with a request for prayer that "God may open to us a door for the word, to declare the mystery of Christ, on account of which I am in prison—that I may make it clear, which is how I ought to speak" (4:3–4). And he counsels the Colossians, "Walk in wisdom toward outsiders, making the best use of the time. Let your speech always be gracious, seasoned with salt, so that you may

---

31 So Harris, *Slave of Christ*, 61–68.

32 Harris, *Slave of Christ*, 139. He also observes that "whereas in many parts of the English-speaking world slavery is part of our history, in the Mediterranean lands of the first century, slavery was a part of their life. This difference is a ground, I submit, not for the purging of the language of slavery from the New Testament, but for its preservation. That is, if the language of slavery is offensive, the offence would have been considerably greater for those who lived in societies where slavery was intrinsic than for us for whom slavery is simply an unpleasant and embarrassing memory." Harris, *Slave of Christ*, 45.

33 For this point, I am indebted to Harris, *Slave of Christ*, 62.

know how you ought to answer each person" (4:5–6). In the context of Colossians, to "walk in wisdom" is to walk in Christ (cf. 2:6), and Paul especially urges us to have the gracious speech of Christ that corresponds with and thus commends God's gracious redemption in Christ.

Conclusion

So it turns out that the theological teaching that "your life is hidden with Christ in God" (3:3) is not esoteric and impractical. On the contrary, our new life in the ascended Christ is the basis upon which Paul instructs the Colossians to put to death the vices of their earthly lives and put on the gentleness and love of Christ. Because of the preeminence and sufficiency of Christ, believers can do all things in his name, even in the most difficult of circumstances, knowing that the final inheritance will come when he is revealed. In the next chapter we see a stunning example of how this hope of the gospel worked out practically in Colossae.

Hope for Philemon and Onesimus

Receive him as you would receive me.

PHILEMON 17

PAUL'S SHORTEST LETTER DEMONSTRATES how the hidden hope of Christ was sufficient for a particularly difficult circumstance in Colossae—the estrangement of Philemon from his slave Onesimus. The gospel gave Philemon hope for growth in the love of Christ. It gave Onesimus a new life in Christ. And it gave them both hope for reconciliation in Christ.

Theology in Philemon?

Some have questioned whether there is any theology in Philemon. Fitzmyer observes, "Because the Letter to Philemon seemed to lack any doctrinal content, it was at times neglected in the ancient church."[1] And Petersen observes that in the modern study of Paul, Philemon "has usually been found uninteresting because of its lack of 'theological' content in comparison with others of Paul's letters."[2] In contrast,

---

1   Joseph A. Fitzmyer, *The Letter to Philemon*, AB (New York: Doubleday, 2000), 8.
2   Norman R. Petersen, *Rediscovering Paul: Philemon and the Sociology of Paul's Narrative World* (Philadelphia: Fortress, 1985), 200. Petersen agrees that it lacks theology but disagrees that this makes it uninteresting.

Wolter has argued that Philemon "demonstrates the ethical impact of Paul's theological thinking."[3] And Wright sees its subversive message of reconciliation in Christ as at the heart of Paul's theology.[4]

I very much agree that there is theology in the letter. But its theology tends to be implicit, as several scholars have observed.[5] There is nothing in Philemon like the profound poem about Christ in Colossians 1:15–20. The focus of this letter is on practical, domestic, and ordinary matters. Still, for Paul, as Luther observes, "one can say nothing so ordinary that Christ is not present."[6] Christ indeed is very present in Philemon as the one *from whom* grace comes (Philem. 3, 25), the one *in whom* believers live (8, 16, 20) and the one *for whom* we live (1, 6, 9). God the Father is also present (3–4), although he is often behind the scenes directing in providence (15) and answering prayers (22).[7] Christ is more prominent in Philemon, as he is in Colossians. He is our Lord and the object of our faith. And he is the one who was knitting Paul, Onesimus, and Philemon together in love.[8]

---

3   Michael Wolter, "The Letter to Philemon as Ethical Counterpart of Paul's Doctrine of Justification," in *Philemon in Perspective: Interpreting a Pauline Letter*, ed. D. Francois Tolmie (New York: De Gruyter, 2010), 178.

4   N. T. Wright, *Paul and the Faithfulness of God* (Minneapolis: Fortress, 2013), 1:3–22.

5   "There is an enormous amount of theological substance in Paul's letter to Philemon, but the theological dimensions of the text are essentially implicit" (Marion L. Soards, "Some Neglected Theological Dimensions of Paul's Letter to Philemon," *PRSt* 17 [1990]: 209–19). "The christology of the letter to Philemon is implied rather than expressly stated." Ralph P. Martin, "The Christology of the Prison Epistles," in *Contours of Christology in the New Testament*, ed. Richard N. Longenecker (Grand Rapids, MI: Eerdmans, 2005), 209.

6   Martin Luther, *Luther's Works*, ed. Jaroslav Pelikan (St. Louis, MO: Concordia, 1968), 29:93.

7   The passive verbs in Philemon—"was parted" (*echōisthē*, 15) and "will be graciously given" (*charisthēsomai*, 22)—are often called "theological passives" because they imply that God is the one acting.

8   Still observes that Christ is mentioned eleven times in Philemon and comments, "Christ stands at the center of [Paul's] theology. In Philemon, Christ is not merely a literary motif woven throughout the letter—he is the one that binds Paul to both Philemon and Onesimus. Paul was convinced that Christ could bring believers together, even a slave and a master." Todd D. Still, "Pauline Theology and Ancient Slavery: Does the Former Support or Subvert the Latter?" *HBT* 27 (2005): 25.

Hope for Philemon

The gospel gave Philemon hope for growth in the love of Christ through reconciliation with his slave Onesimus. Paul wrote this letter as an appeal for Philemon to welcome back his estranged slave. He carefully navigates his way toward this appeal in Philemon 8–21, finally coming to the main point in verse 17: "So if you consider me your partner, receive him as you would receive me." Paul roots this appeal in the fruit of faith and love that the gospel was bearing in Philemon's life (4–7). He both thanks God for this fruit and prays that Philemon would grow more in it by welcoming back Onesimus.[9]

Paul knew firsthand of Philemon's faith, for he had been instrumental in Philemon's conversion. In his appeal, he reminds Philemon that he had saved his very life through the gospel: "to say nothing of your owing me even your own self" (19). This probably happened during Paul's long ministry in Ephesus on the third missionary journey. Here Paul thanks God, however, not for Philemon's initial coming to faith but for his persevering faith that Paul was hearing about from Epaphras or perhaps even from Onesimus.[10] Philemon was continuing in the faith, "stable and steadfast, not shifting from the hope of the gospel that [he] heard" (Col. 1:23).

Philemon's faith was fundamentally oriented "toward the Lord Jesus" (Philem. 5). Some commentators argue that the word order of this verse indicates that Paul means Philemon's faith or faithfulness was directed toward both the Lord and the saints:[11] "I hear of your love and of the faith[fulness] that you have toward the Lord Jesus and

---

9 Calvin comments, "It should be noted that he prays for the very same people for whom he gives thanks. Even the most perfect men who deserve the highest praise need to be prayed for, as long as they live in the world, that God would grant them not only to persevere to the end but also to make progress day by day." John Calvin, *The Second Epistle of Paul the Apostle to the Corinthians and the Epistles to Timothy, Titus and Philemon*, trans. T. A. Smail (1964; repr., Grand Rapids, MI: Eerdmans, 1976), 394.

10 In Col. 1:4, Paul's thanksgiving uses the aorist participle "since we heard" (*akousantes*). But in Philem. 5 he uses the present participle "because I hear" (*akouōn*), probably indicating that he continues to hear encouraging reports about his friend in Colossae.

11 For example, G. K. Beale, *Colossians and Philemon*, BECNT (Grand Rapids, MI: Baker Academic, 2019), 385–87.

for all the saints" (5). But the parallel thanksgivings in Paul's other letters present faith as directed toward Christ and love toward the saints (Eph. 1:15–16; Col. 1:3–4). So it makes better sense to see Paul communicating this truth through a chiasm:[12]

> I hear of your love
>> and of the faith
>> that you have toward the Lord Jesus
> and for all the saints.

Perhaps Paul places Philemon's faith at the heart of the chiasm because his faith in the Lord was the foundation of his new life in Christ.

His faith in the Lord also drew him together into partnership with other believers, a point that is fundamental to Paul's appeal for reconciliation: "So if you consider me your *partner*, receive him as you would receive me" (Philem. 17). The word translated "partner" (*koinōnon*) is related to the word translated "sharing" (*koinōnia*) in Philemon 6. This is a key verse in Paul's argument, but unfortunately it is difficult to translate. In my view, "your partnership with us in the faith" (NIV) is a better translation than "the sharing of your faith" (ESV). Paul's point is not about evangelism but about how our common faith in the Lord draws us together into "partnership." Paul and Philemon were partners in the faith, and now the formerly estranged slave Onesimus has been wrapped into this partnership as well.

Another way to speak of this partnership is our love for one another. Our common faith binds us together into a family of "brothers" and "sisters" (1, 2, 7, 20) who are "beloved" to one another (1). In fact, the emphasis of Paul's opening thanksgiving is on Philemon's love. This is probably why he uses the chiasm—Paul typically thanks God for his readers' faith before their love (Eph. 1:15; Col. 1:4; 1 Thess. 1:3; 2 Thess. 1:3); but in Philemon he thanks God first for Philemon's love (Philem. 5), which envelops the faith from which it derives. Paul also

---

12   So BDF §477.2.

emphasizes Philemon's love in the closing verse of his prayer: "For I have derived much joy and comfort from your love, my brother" (7). The reason for this emphasis is that love is "the characteristic which is of supreme importance for the appeal which is to follow."[13]

Philemon's love was directed toward "*all* the saints" (5). The clearest example of his love was his hospitality in welcoming a church in his house (2), perhaps the whole church at Colossae. Paul had probably also seen Philemon's love for many different people in Ephesus. And perhaps he was hearing reports of Philemon's love for saints in neighboring cities like Laodicea. Finally, "all the saints" may mean that Philemon's love did not discriminate between believers who were Greek or Jew, slave or free (cf. Col. 3:11). Much of this paragraph is speculation, but one thing is certain: the hearts of the saints had been refreshed through the love of Philemon (Philem. 7).

Still, like all of us, Philemon had room to grow and increase in his love. Paul wanted to see God bear more fruit in Philemon's life. He prays "that your partnership with us in the faith may be effective" (6 NIV). What counts in Christ is "faith working [*energoumenē*] through love" (Gal. 5:6), and here Paul prays that Philemon's faith would once again work or be "effective [*energēs*]" in love. Specifically, Paul prays that Philemon's faith would be effective "for the full knowledge of every good thing that is in us for the sake of Christ" (Philem. 6). The knowledge of God and his will is both the root and the goal of walking in Christ (Col. 1:9–10). So Paul prays that Philemon would grow in this knowledge. Even more specifically, the object of this knowledge is "*every* good thing" that Philemon should do.[14] Philemon's love should not only reach *all* the saints; it should include *all* the good acts of love that God would have him do.

Paul is subtly introducing the main appeal of his letter that he states explicitly in Philemon 17. At one point he speaks similarly of

---

13 Karl P. Donfried and I. Howard Marshall, *The Theology of the Shorter Pauline Epistles* (New York: Cambridge University Press, 1993), 182.

14 Beale insightfully observes the parallel of "every good thing" in Philem. 6 and "every good work" in Col. 1:10. *Colossians and Philemon*, 389.

the "good deed" that Philemon should do (14 CSB). His focus on Philemon's love in the opening prayer is the ground for his appeal in the rest of the letter. Philemon needed to grow in his love by showing this love to Onesimus, who was now his "beloved brother" (16). Just as he had refreshed the hearts of the saints in the past (7), so now he must refresh Paul's heart by showing love to Onesimus, welcoming him back and forgiving him (17–20), as the Lord had forgiven him (cf. Col. 3:13).[15]

It is striking how Paul practiced what he preached in his pastoral approach in this letter. As an apostle, Paul could have commanded Philemon, but instead he appealed to him from a position of humility: "Though I am bold enough in Christ to command you to do what is required, yet for love's sake I prefer to appeal to you—I, Paul, an old man and now a prisoner also for Christ Jesus" (Philem. 8). Paul also set aside his own desires, submitting them to Philemon's consent: "I would have been glad to keep him with me, in order that he might serve me on your behalf during my imprisonment for the gospel, but I preferred to do nothing without your consent in order that your goodness might not be by compulsion but of your own accord" (13–14). And he stood in the place of Onesimus, promising to pay Philemon all his debts: "If he has wronged you at all, or owes you anything, charge that to my account. I, Paul, write this with my own hand: I will repay it" (18–19).[16] Paul's approach in this letter is not simply a matter of strategy but of theology. Paul knew that love is a fruit produced by God's Spirit in the lives of believers because of the hope they have in Christ. So he sought to tend the garden of Philemon's heart through Christian persuasion

---

15 Williams observes that this story "shows us that forgiveness is a mark of the people of God." Jarvis J. Williams, *Redemptive Kingdom Diversity: A Biblical Theology of the People of God* (Grand Rapids, MI: Baker Academic, 2021), 131.

16 Luther saw here an illustration of the love of Christ for us (Eduard Lohse, *Colossians and Philemon*, Hermeneia, trans. William R. Poehlmann and Robert J. Karris [Philadelphia: Fortress, 1971], 188). And Calvin was struck by Paul's humility: "On behalf of a man of the lowest condition he condescends to such modesty and humility that hardly anywhere else do we have such a living picture of the meekness of his character." *Second Epistle of Paul*, 393.

rather than through enforcement.[17] He showed the love of Christ to Philemon with the goal that Philemon would do the same to Onesimus.

Hope for Onesimus

Onesimus was a slave, the lowest of social circumstances. His name meant "useful," a common name given to slaves in the ancient world; but Paul tells Philemon that "he was *useless* to you" (11). He had most likely run away from Philemon and stolen from him (18). Paul may be thinking that the act of running away was theft, since a slave did not even own himself. Or perhaps Onesimus had also stolen to have the means of getting away.[18] In any event, this had created a great tension between Philemon and Onesimus, which is clear from the very careful way that Paul makes his appeal to welcome him back. Surely Onesimus came back to Colossae with some trepidation.

But he also came back with hope. For in Christ he had been given new life and thus a reason for hope. First, the gospel had given Onesimus a new birth. Paul describes him as "my child . . . whose father I became in my imprisonment" (10). More literally, the Greek says, "who I bore in my imprisonment," describing Paul's role in Onesimus's conversion or new birth.[19] Onesimus had come to believe in Christ. Second, the gospel had given Onesimus a new name: "Formerly he was useless to you, but now he is indeed useful to you and to me" (11). In Christ, Onesimus could now live up to his name: Useful. He had taken

---

17 Thielman observes, "If necessary, Paul could issue authoritative directives about how his churches should conduct themselves. At the same time he seems to have believed that Christian ethical behavior should arise from the individual's own inner convictions. Perhaps his understanding of the new covenant as a covenant whose stipulations are written on the heart has led him to this position." Frank Thielman, *Theology of the New Testament: A Canonical and Synthetic Approach* (Grand Rapids, MI: Zondervan, 2005), 390.

18 Cf. Epictetus: "How do [runaway slaves], when they run off, leave their masters? . . . Don't they steal just a little bit to last them for the first few days, and then afterwards drift along over land or sea, contriving one scheme after another to keep themselves fed?" *Diatr.* 3.26.

19 For fatherhood as a metaphor for Paul's role in conversion, see 1 Cor. 4:15, 17; and Gal. 4:19.

off the old man and put on the new man.[20] Perhaps the words "useless" (*achrēstos*) and "useful" (*euchrēstos*) are also a play on his former life without Christ (a-Christ) and his new life of usefulness in Christ. He had been given a new name. Third, the gospel had given Onesimus a new family. In Colossians Paul speaks of Onesimus as "our faithful and beloved *brother*" (Col. 4:9) and in Philemon as "my very heart" (Philem. 12) and as Philemon's "beloved *brother*" (16).

All of this (11–16) is the reason Paul concludes with his hopeful appeal in Philemon 17. But one statement stands out as the "theological highpoint" of the letter:[21] "For this perhaps is why he was parted from you for a while, that you might have him back forever, no longer as a [slave] but more than a [slave], as a beloved brother—especially to me, but how much more to you, both in the flesh and in the Lord" (15–16).[22] Paul sees God's kind providence behind the difficult departure of Onesimus. God's ultimate goal was not separation but reunion—an *eternal* reunion in fact ("forever"), as well as a *family* reunion ("as a beloved brother"). They were separated momentarily that they might be joined forever in a much closer relationship. And the basis of all of this was the Lord Jesus, the object of their (now) mutual faith. This is probably what Paul means when he says "both in the flesh and in the Lord": not only would Onesimus and Philemon be reunited physically "in the flesh"; they would be reunited spiritually "in the Lord."[23] This was surely a reason for Onesimus to hope.

Philemon 16 contains an "egalitarian statement" similar to what we saw in Colossians: in the new man "there is not Greek and Jew, circumcised and uncircumcised, barbarian, Scythian, slave, free; but

---

20 Beale observes that Philem. 11 has bearing on the distinction between the old and new man and the old and new creation. *Colossians and Philemon*, 406–7.

21 Douglas J. Moo, *The Letters to the Colossians and to Philemon*, PNTC (Grand Rapids, MI: Eerdmans, 2008), 425n104.

22 I have changed the ESV's translation "bondservant" to "slave" in Philem. 16. For my reasoning, see p. 81n21.

23 I am taking "in the flesh and in the Lord" as modifying the verb "you might have him back" in Philem. 15. Most interpreters, however, take these phrases as modifying "brother" in Philem. 16 and it explain it variously as "in the home and in the church" or as "on an earthly level and on a spiritual level."

Christ is all, and in all" (Col. 3:11). I argued in the last chapter that we must understand this statement in a relative sense rather than an absolute sense, because Paul continues to uphold the social conditions of Christian slaves in the household code (Col. 3:22–4:1). Believers must continue to live in the differing social conditions in which they are called, but these differences are relativized in the church. Similarly, in this context, the statement "no longer as a slave" (Philem. 16) must be taken as a relative rather than an absolute statement. In what sense would Philemon receive Onesimus back "no longer as a slave"? In the sense that he is "more than a slave . . . a beloved brother." So Paul does not explicitly call for Onesimus's emancipation in this verse.[24] We should not overstate this clarification, however, and miss the point Paul is making: Onesimus is now Philemon's brother! He has a new social standing in Christ, an equal standing in the church with his master Philemon. An example of this new social standing is the way Paul presents Onesimus on the same level as Tychicus, the man who carried these letters to Colossae, for both are identified as faithful and as beloved brothers (Col. 4:7, 9).

Freedom from Slavery?

Many interpreters argue further that Paul subtly and implicitly appeals to Philemon to release Onesimus from slavery. In Philemon 13–14, Paul mentions that he would have preferred for Onesimus to stay and minister to him in his imprisonment, but he did not want to do this without Philemon's consent. This implies that he wanted Philemon not only to welcome Onesimus but to then send him back to Paul, and some suggest this further implies Onesimus's freedom. In the egalitarian statement of Philemon 16, many see the death knell of the institution

---

24 *Pace* Stephen E. Young, *Our Brother Beloved: Purpose and Community in Paul's Letter to Philemon* (Waco, TX: Baylor University Press, 2021), 133. Young suggests that it would be basically impossible for Philemon to consider Onesimus both a brother and a slave (*Our Beloved Brother*, 134). But this was apparently not impossible in the ancient world, for Sirach advises masters both to discipline their slaves and to treat them as brothers (Sir. 33:25–33). It should be noted, however, that Paul's teaching goes beyond Sirach in arguing that Onesimus actually *is* Philemon's brother in the Lord.

of slavery, captured well by Bruce's vivid statement: "What this letter does is to bring us into an atmosphere in which the institution could only wilt and die."[25] And in Philemon 21 Paul offers this tantalizing statement: "Confident of your obedience, I write to you, knowing that you will do *even more* than I say." What is the more? Sending him back? Freeing him? Or perhaps Paul had nothing specific in mind?

I observed in the prologue that Onesimus's enslavement is probably the most pressing issue for modern Christians who read this letter. It was surely a pressing issue for Onesimus as well, especially if he had run away to gain his freedom. But it is pressing for us today because of the existence and abolition of slavery in the modern world. Almost every Christian today would agree that slavery is wrong and was rightly abolished. But in the decades leading up to the American Civil War Christians disagreed intensely with one another on the issue, and, not surprisingly, in their interpretation of Scripture.[26] Philemon tended to be used in support of slavery, especially by those who defended the Fugitive Slave Act of 1850.[27] In contrast, radical abolitionists in America tended to ignore or reject Scripture altogether and argue that slavery was a "sin in itself" based upon liberal Enlightenment principles. More orthodox Christians who supported abolition argued that slavery should be abolished because Scripture condemned the specific form of slavery as it existed in the modern world, based as it was in theft, racism, sexual abuse, and cruelty. This is the position advocated, for example, by John Newton, who wrote an influential account of the evils of the African slave trade.[28]

25 F. F. Bruce, *Paul: Apostle of the Heart Set Free* (Grand Rapids, MI: Eerdmans, 1977), 401.

26 For this paragraph, I am deeply indebted to Mark A. Noll, *The Civil War as a Theological Crisis* (Chapel Hill: The University of North Carolina Press, 2006); and Robert Bruce Mullin, "Biblical Critics and the Battle over Slavery," *Journal of Presbyterian History (1962–1985)* 61.2 (1983): 210–26.

27 For a well-researched introduction to uses of Philemon in the polemics leading up to the Civil War, see Young, *Our Beloved Brother*, 7–23.

28 For the story of Newton's influential *Thoughts upon the African Slave Trade*, see Jonathan Aitken, *John Newton: From Disgrace to Amazing Grace* (Wheaton, IL: Crossway, 2007), 319–28.

How then should we as Christians think about Philemon in light of the existence and abolition of slavery in the modern world? First, we should see that Philemon does not in fact support the African slave trade or slavery as it existed in America, which violated the law of God on so many counts. Second, we should remember that Scripture does tolerate and regulate slavery, even though it cuts against God's design in creation.[29] This will help us understand why Paul did not simply command Philemon to free Onesimus. Third, we should remember Paul's counsel to slaves to gain their freedom if they can (1 Cor. 7:21). In light of this, it is very possible that he was subtly persuading Philemon to release Onesimus. Fourth, we should question the absolute value placed upon freedom in the modern world, for Paul's main goal was not Onesimus's freedom but his reconciliation with Philemon.[30]

Reconciliation

The hope of the newly converted Onesimus as he returned to Colossae was that he would be reconciled with Philemon. Reconciliation is the reason Paul wrote on his behalf, appealing to Philemon to "receive him as you would receive me" (Philem. 17). The verb "receive" means to "extend a welcome."[31] It is the same verb Paul uses several times in Romans 14–15, where he urges Jewish and Gentile Christians in Rome to "welcome one another as Christ has welcomed you, for the glory of God" (Rom. 15:7). In these passages we see the important role of hospitality in the church, extending welcome to those with whom we disagree and even to those who have wronged us in the past. We are reminded of Paul's words to the whole church in Colossae: "Put on then, as God's chosen ones, holy and beloved, compassionate hearts, kindness, humility, meekness, and patience, bearing with one another

---

29 For a discussion of slavery in biblical theology, see pp. 83–85.

30 Wright poignantly observes, "For Philemon to have responded angrily to Paul's letter by giving Onesimus his freedom but declaring that he never wanted to set eyes on him again would have meant defeat for Paul." *Paul and the Faithfulness of God*, 12.

31 BDAG, s.v., "*proslambanō*," use 4.

and, if one has a complaint against another, forgiving each other; as the Lord has forgiven you, so you also must forgive" (Col. 3:12–13).

Many have observed that Philemon works out the theology of cosmic reconciliation in Colossians on a horizontal level.[32] The reconciliation of all things has already been accomplished through and for the Son—peace has been made "by the blood of his cross" (Col. 1:20). Now we must let this peace rule in our hearts (Col. 3:15). We must live out this new life here on earth by welcoming one another.[33] This is what Paul was laboring to persuade Philemon to do—to bridge the gap between what is true in Christ (the indicative) and what ought to be true in Christ (the imperative), all "for the sake of Christ" (Philem. 6).[34]

Walking in Christ is not easy. The broken relationship between Philemon and Onesimus is one grain of sand in a desert of conflict found in a world at conflict with God. Paul was no idealist when it came to pursuing peace with others: "If possible, so far as it depends on you, live peaceably with all" (Rom. 12:18). But he also knew that in the Lord his labor to reconcile Philemon and Onesimus was not in vain (cf. 1 Cor. 15:58), for God had already made peace in the cross, and he is making peace through the proclamation of his Son around the world. Therefore, no one is without hope, and we should never give up hope.[35] Christ may be currently hidden. But he is preeminent and sufficient, and he will one day be revealed.

Conclusion

The theology of Philemon is more implicit than the theology of Colossians, but without it Philemon and Onesimus would have been without

---

32 For example, Thielman, *New Testament Theology*, 389; Martin, "Christology," 209.

33 Wright concludes, "No Christian has a right to refuse a welcome to one whom God has welcomed. Faith in Christ, the basis of justification, is the basis also of *koinōnia* ["partnership"]. Justification by faith must result in fellowship by faith." N. T. Wright, *Colossians and Philemon: An Introduction and Commentary*, TNTC (Downers Grove, IL: InterVarsity Press, 1986), 193.

34 Just as Col. 1:20 speaks of Christ as the goal or final cause of reconciliation (*eis Christon*), so does Philem. 6 (*eis auton*).

35 See Luther's conclusion from the story of Onesimus: "Thus no one ought to despair about anyone else. . . . On the basis of this example we should not despair either about ourselves or our brethren." *Luther's Works*, 29:94.

hope. Philemon's faith in the Lord Jesus gave him hope for growth in the love of Christ by reconciling with Onesimus. And Onesimus's new birth, new name, and new family gave him hope that Paul's appeal would be successful—that he and Philemon would be reconciled as brothers in Christ. Thus the hidden hope of Christ was sufficient for this difficult earthly circumstance.

Epilogue

Hope for Paul

WRITING FROM PRISON, Paul instructs Philemon, "Prepare a guest room for me, for I am hoping that through your prayers I will be graciously given to you" (Philem. 22). In this side comment we gain insight into the reason Paul had confidence for the future even in the midst of the difficult circumstances of these letters. His hope was in God, the one who answers our prayers, and in the grace of God, the one who graciously gives us all things (Rom. 8:32).

The gospel Paul and Epaphras proclaimed is a message about the grace of God in Christ (Col. 1:6). God has redeemed us in his Son and is reconciling all things through him and for him. The Son of God is the revelation of God, the image of God, the fullness of God, and the wisdom of God. He is preeminent in everything, and he is sufficient for everything in our lives. Believers have been buried with him in baptism and raised with him to new life. Further, our lives are hidden with him in God and will be revealed with him in the glory of the resurrection. Christ is our life, and his resurrection life is manifest in us here and now as the gospel bears fruit in our lives, just as it was doing in the lives of Philemon and Onesimus, not to mention Paul. A decade before writing this letter Paul had come into conflict with Barnabas over whether to take Mark on the second missionary journey (Acts 16:36–41), but in these letters we see that Paul and Mark have been reconciled (Col. 4:10; Philem. 24).

So how did it all turn out in Colossae? We know almost nothing about what happened in the church of Colossae after these letters were written. Most think that Philemon and Onesimus were reconciled, because otherwise the letter to Philemon would not have been preserved. And most in the history of the church have thought that Paul was released from his first Roman imprisonment. Perhaps he even visited Philemon in Colossae as he had hoped? There is a lot we don't know. But we do know that even where things did not work out so well, Paul's hope was in heaven. His hope transcended his earthly circumstances because his hope was in Christ, and thus his hope was in God.

General Index

Scripture Index

New Testament Theology

Edited by Thomas R. Schreiner and Brian S. Rosner, this series presents clear, scholarly overviews of the main theological themes of each book of the New Testament, examining what they reveal about God and his relation to the world in the context of the overarching biblical narrative.

For more information, visit **crossway.org**.